FEATHERBEDDING AND JOB SECURITY

FEATHERBEDDING AND JOB SECURITY

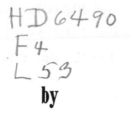
by

Robert D. Leiter

73414

TWAYNE PUBLISHERS, INC.   •   NEW YORK

PREFACE

Early in 1959, when I first decided to undertake a study of featherbedding, railroad carriers were girding for what appeared to be a serious struggle with the unions. I contemplated looking into some of the prevalent work practices which had come to the attention of the public from time to time and had generally aroused criticism and condemnation. The causes of so much waste of resources and the means by which objectionable union rules and work practices could be eliminated seemed to be matters well worth investigating.

Immersion in these problems soon indicated that the task was far larger than I had anticipated. Ramifications of many kinds became apparent, and it seemed advisable to expand the scope of the study on featherbedding in order to make possible a clearer understanding of all that is involved. This monograph, therefore, examines those facets of technological change which are necessary to understand the role of job and economic security in the attitudes and activities of labor. It attempts to give a comprehensive and systematic analysis of those matters, a project I felt was in order.

Much of the profuse literature dealing with featherbedding is superficial, and little attempt has been made to define terms rigorously or uniformly. Each author tends to use his own concepts to determine appropriate and relevant subject matter. It is this difficulty which led me to select and emphasize the one recurring thread which pervades all discussions of featherbedding: Work practices that stem from fear of displacement provide unnecessary work or yield unearned wages. Workers are trying to protect their jobs; on the other hand, employers are fighting to establish management prerogatives.

Basic to the development of featherbedding are fear of displacement and resistance to machinery. Featherbedding grew out of an environment of violence in which destruction of machinery was frequent; it represents a more civilized way in which workers may protect their employment opportunities. Since the plight of workers affected by technological change concerns many groups in the economy, different attitudes toward displacement and featherbedding are examined in this study. Featherbedding, it will be shown, is not as widespread as is often alleged. It is limited almost entirely to the transportation, construction, entertainment, and printing industries. But the economic cost of featherbedding and makework is difficult to assess, and only extremely rough estimates are available. In any event, such figures hardly take account of human values, which, of course, are the prime consideration in dealing with displacement.

Following the discussion of the different attitudes is an analysis of the development and current role of featherbedding in the four industries where it chiefly occurs. Gradual relaxation of rigid work rules has been the general practice within these industries. Outside of prohibiting a few limited and very crude manifestations of featherbedding, however, the law has not succeeded in enacting any changes. But this is probably as it should be, since other means of eliminating undesirable union practices seem preferable. For that matter, neither should protection of unnecessary jobs be a function of the law.

What stands out clearly is that featherbedding is part of the larger problem of technological displacement. As industrial and governmental techniques and programs reduce the fears which workers have of new machinery, featherbedding will also decline. It is true that craft unionism must bear some of the blame for makework, but generally the best method of ridding industry of featherbedding is to tackle the overall problems of displacement and to increase job security.

The chief sources of materials for this monograph were the publications of management and labor unions, articles by independent observers and reporters, and investigations and documents by governmental agencies and legislative bodies. Some of the more useful items are included in the bibliography, but these represent only a small fraction of the number read. In addition, I interviewed many persons in different walks of life who were familiar with various aspects of featherbedding. They contributed greatly to my understanding of the issues involved and showed me ramifications which are not ordinarily evident. To all these people I owe a debt of gratitude.

Several of my professional colleagues were especially helpful. Professor Jacob Mincer of Columbia University not only provided me with some valuable insights, but also read the full draft of the manuscript and made a number of good suggestions. Professors William I. Greenwald and Benjamin J. Klebaner of the City College of the City University of New York also read the entire manuscript, and each gave me the benefit of his scholarship. To all three of these men I express my grateful thanks. And to Mrs. Elsa Loewenstein, a graduate student at the City College of the City University of New York, I express my gratitude for her research assistance in gathering the bibliography.

R. D. L.

CITY COLLEGE OF THE CITY UNIVERSITY OF NEW YORK

April 1, 1964

CONTENTS

9

10

Chapter I

TECHNOLOGICAL CHANGE: THE
BACKGROUND OF FEATHERBEDDING

Workers almost instinctively have always feared the introduction of machinery into the productive process. Even when mechanical contrivances have reduced the arduousness of labor, sentiment has been dominated by the idea that employment opportunities would contract, technological unemployment would occur, skills would be displaced, or wages would decline. Only recently has serious thought been given to the validity of this attitude. Careful theoretical analysis of the impact of technology on labor did not begin until the early part of the nineteenth century. Governmental concern in the United States developed even later but, as a result, many investigations of the problem by the legislative and executive branches of the federal government were undertaken. Today, the controversy regarding the effects of technological change on employment still rages.

HISTORY OF RESISTANCE TO TECHNOLOGICAL CHANGE

Most changes which affect human society encounter opposition. Men resist innovation for a variety of reasons. They may have vested interests in the established relationships and routines; they may each have different objectives; they may fear the difficulties which will arise from the impact of new methods, including the disturbance of habits which have created a sense of psychological equilibrium;

11

they may suffer from inertia and lethargy; or they may be
prejudiced. Such behavior has marked the history of civilization.

Primitive societies are not static, but neither are they hos-
pitable to growth. The rate of economic change in those
environments is slowed by the relative isolation which limits
contacts and interchanges with other groups, by the concentration of power among the older members of the body,
by the small technological base upon which to build, by
the limited extent of division of labor, and by the absence
of surplus resources which permit experimentation and risk.
Many of these factors have also been prevalent in rural
regions.

The ancient world was subject to similar factors, but
technological progress was further limited. Labor was
usually plentiful, manual and skilled work was considered
degrading, and the search for practical applications was
shunned as being outside the scope of science. The Middle
Ages were no more predisposed to encourage technological
progress. The economic and social stratifications of society
sanctioned by the Church and feudal hierarchy were not
conducive to change. Because experimentation, innovation,
and the accumulation of wealth by individuals were frowned
upon, technology advanced very little during the period.
Only with the advent of capitalism and the glorification of
profits did there develop a clear incentive for invention.
Nevertheless impediments were present. In addition to some
of the obstacles which had existed in ancient civilizations,
there were several new ones. The guilds opposed changes
in the ways of making things, the landed aristocracy resisted
the growing power of merchants and industrialists, the
patent monopolists who had been established through sov-
ereign power shunned new techniques, the industrial monopolists struggled against competitors, and the workers lived
in fear of displacement.

Consider such conditions as they compare to those in
recent times. Modern technological progress has been fought
not only by workers and unions, but by governments, em-

ployers, farmers, and professional persons. The reception of technological change, therefore, can be seen to depend on the state of the economy, the social structure of the society, and the various psychological, governmental, and religious factors prevailing at the time. Careful and detailed documentation of opposition to the advance of technology since the thirteenth century is available. Difficulties encountered in instituting new devices and techniques in transportation, communication, power generation, metallurgy, textile milling, agriculture, and building processes have been fully described.[1] Permanent and temporary suppression of inventions have been commonplace occurrences.

The Industrial Revolution of the late eighteenth century, which introduced power machinery and the factory system, eliminated much household production and caused the separation of management from labor. The beginning of the twentieth century brought assembly line and mass production techniques into being. Very expensive machinery forced a division between the ownership and management of business enterprise. The decade of the 1940's opened up an era of automation in which automatic controls and decisions made by electronic devices without human intervention have integrated production on much vaster scales in the factory and office. Early mechanization replaced human and animal muscle by machinery; more recently, work done with human senses and brainpower has been take over by machines. Each major technological development has brought new problems for labor.

Not all resistance to new industrial techniques has come from employees. Employers and the government, both in Great Britain and on the European continent, have sometimes acted to preserve the jobs of workers. For a long time workers reacted slowly. Clear-cut opposition of labor to technological advance became pronounced with the advent of the factory system and the Industrial Revolution, when wages typically had become the sole means of support. Widespread and more rapid introduction of machinery in the British textile industry during the eighteenth century

caused much distress among skilled craftsmen. Many of
these skilled workers lost their employment; others sus-
tained a deterioration of wages and conditions of work
under the competitive pressures in the industry. Labor was
gravely concerned with industrial change and there were
numerous manifestations of an attitude of hostility by some
of those whose livelihoods were periled. Wrecking machinery ordinarily occurred spontaneously and by nonunion
workers.

The destruction of machinery was an important factor
in British economic life between some indeterminate point
in the seventeenth century until about 1830.[2] It had three
different aspects. Some of the havoc was only an incidental phase of riots against high prices and other matters of
dissatisfaction which occurred from time to time. A much
more significant type of wrecking represented pressure by
workers against employers rather than particular hostility to
machinery. In a period when unionism was weak, strike
funds low, and strikebreakers readily available, machine
breaking was an effective and normal weapon in preventing
a plant from operating, at least temporarily. It could be
used for this purpose, however, only when occasional pressure had to be exerted on employers, as in those cases where
working conditions were abruptly changed. Textile workers,
miners, and seamen were among the most frequent users
of this technique. Machine wrecking was obviously less
useful when a more permanent constraining force against
employers was necessary. Wrecking as a general device
served to insure greater solidarity among the workers and
strengthened their bargaining position. It was an established
and traditional part of industrial strife in the early period
of the factory system and, during the same years, in mining
operations.[3] Destruction, directed not only at machinery
but also at raw materials, finished goods, and other property of employers as the situation warranted, provided
much of the basis of the power of workers.

The Luddite activities of the early nineteenth century
generally are included in this type of behavior. Organized

bands of rioters, known as Ludds or Luddites, appeared in Nottingham at the end of 1811, and the following year spread to Derbyshire, Lancashire, Leicestershire, and Yorkshire. The group, which generally operated at night in masks, was led by a man known as "General Ludd" and "King Ludd." He probably derived his name from Ned Ludd, an idiot boy who wrecked some stocking frames in a factory in a fit of temper when he was unable to catch someone who had been annoying him. The riotous mob of manual workers, who destroyed stocking frames, steam power looms, and other textile machinery and occasionally demolished factories in efforts to improve working conditions, was supported by local public opinion. But repressive government measures followed. The movement was temporarily brought to an end in 1813 through a mass trial in York which led to the hanging and transportation of a large number of persons convicted of statutory violations. The labor movement, however, generally supported the Luddites. Evidence of a direct connection between those found guilty in these cases and the Luddites is uncertain.[4]

The deep depression following the conclusion of the Napoleonic Wars led to a resumption, in 1816, of organized rioting and destruction of industrial equipment which extended almost throughout the whole of Great Britain. Severe repressive measures and improving economic conditions terminated the activities of the Luddites shortly thereafter.

The activities of the Luddites in particular and the wrecking of machinery generally evoked wide interest. The opposition of George Gordon, Lord Byron to a bill subsequently enacted which made the willful destruction of stocking frames a capital offense was brilliantly expressed in his maiden speech to the House of Lords in 1812.[5] Charlotte Bronte's *Shirley*, published in 1849, includes an account of riots caused by the displacement of hand labor by machinery.[6]

Such tactics by workers have persisted to the present day. A well-known recent illustration of willful destruction of ma-

chinery to support collective bargaining demands occurred
in 1937 during a strike at the Apex Hosiery Company in
Philadelphia, Pennsylvania.[7]

The third type of wrecking was aimed specifically at
machines which were causing unemployment, reducing the
standard of living, limiting freedom, and stifling dignity.
Devices which did not adversely affect workers were not
resisted. For example, in the antimachinery riots of 1779,
Lancashire workers broke only spinning jennies of twenty-
four or more spindles, but spared smaller ones.[8] In Great
Britain, the most important cases of destruction of machines
which served as labor-saving equipment involved the shearmen working on finished cloth in 1802, weavers struggling
against power looms in 1826, and farm laborers fighting the
threshing machines in 1830. Another important incident
took place about 1840, when the power loom invented ap-
proximately fifty years earlier superseded the hand loom in
the cotton industry in Manchester, England. Five thousand
weavers, fearing that 3,500 of their number would be displaced with very little possibility of obtaining employment
elsewhere, tried to stop the introduction of the power
loom and forestall its consequences. The weavers burned
down some factories, broke into others to destroy machinery,
and beat strikebreakers who took jobs.[9] Beginning near
the middle of the nineteenth century, however, the general
policy of British trade unions moved in the direction of
accepting and controlling new machinery. Disputes with
employers usually involved questions concerning the need
to change working conditions because of the introduction
of new equipment and techniques.[10]

Workers also evinced much resentment against those persons who revolutionized industrial techniques. As a result
of inventing the flying shuttle in 1733, John Kay had to leave
England. James Hargreaves, who originated the spinning
jenny in 1764, had his machine destroyed by workers four
years later.[11] The mill of Richard Arkwright, inventor of the
water frame and sometimes considered the father of the factory system, was destroyed in 1779 in antimachinery riots.

Samuel Crompton was forced into hiding when he devised the spinning mule in 1779. The violent reaction to these four inventors serves to illustrate the attitude of workers.

During the entire period, opposition to machinery was supported in many instances by the public and by employers themselves. Public sentiment was often sympathetically disposed to workers threatened with displacement. Smaller entrepreneurs and shopkeepers rarely benefited from machinery and even larger capitalists did not always foresee immediate profits in the introduction of new equipment. There was thus much sentiment against innovation even by employers. In France, for example, much of the destruction occurred through the connivance of small shop owners with their employees to destroy machines being introduced by competitors.[12]

Although British workers gradually abandoned the policy of wrecking machines during the nineteenth century, restriction of output was frequently used to voice opposition. As the conflict between employers and employees became extremely bitter toward the close of the century and public discussion of labor issues was more frequent, workers rarely specified limits openly on the amount they would produce. Nevertheless, strong unions did attempt to influence policies of the firm regarding apprenticeship, manning schedules, and wage rates through the process of collective bargaining. And agreements reached in these matters certainly affected the output of the firms involved. During the early 1900's British employers contended that ethical sentiment in that country did not require employees to have a voice in deciding the conditions under which they worked.[13] Nevertheless, the decline in British business and industry was attributed in great measure to the fact that British workers did not do their best. The superiority of United States manufacturing industries to those of Great Britain was ascribed to the discouragement of activity by British unionism.[14]

Widespread public interest in the matter of union restriction of output in Great Britain started in the 1890's in con-

nection with the development by several unions of a policy
known as ca'canny, go canny, or skulk. This technique, used
by unions not strong enough to strike to limit output, related
the effort expended by the worker in production to his
estimate of the fairness of the wage rate. The policy was
adopted officially for the first time in 1891, when the dock
workers took the step.[15] Beginning in 1896, it received new
impetus through the efforts of the union of ship, dock, and
river workers and was popular among British workers in a
number of unions for a short time.[16] Indeed, one of the main
issues in the great strike of British engineers in 1897 concerned limitation of output. But by 1901, the public outcry
against these practices had led British labor leaders to dis-
countenance and try to prevent direct restriction of output.

Nevertheless, criticism of restrictive practices and low
productivity of British labor has continued. A study of
thirteen British industries completed in 1935 concluded that
"our first definite feeling is that the obstructions to industrial efficiency and improvement set up by trade unions are
nothing like so serious as is commonly alleged." [17] Employers, however, have not all accepted this evaluation.

Beginning in 1660, it was largely the attitude of the
British government, which supported and encouraged the
introduction of new machines and techniques stimulating
private enterprise regardless of social cost that was responsible for the successful mechanization of industry.[18] In part,
however, many of the industrial changes were possible
because they were made during periods of prosperity when
resistance by workers was low.

In France, industrialization came much later than in Great
Britain and machinery wrecking was more sporadic and less
effective. But it did occur. Occasional incidents are recorded
as early as 1571. Factory hands destroyed spinning jennies
when they were introduced in 1789.[19] Looms invented
twelve years later by Joseph M. Jacquard to weave brocaded
silks were destroyed by another group of displaced French
workers.[20] The most violent organized outburst was that of
the cloth shearmen in 1819. The threat of the machine was

a vaguer one to French workers, and in most instances French machinery was only competitive to British. In France, too, the destruction of machinery faded in importance after 1830,[21] except as part of syndicalist action.

Experiences in the United States differed from those in Great Britain and on the Continent. American labor was more mobile and had greater economic opportunities, so that disposition to wreck machinery for fear of unemployment was extremely rare. Generally, machinery was introduced into an economy which was expanding and dynamic, and workers were not faced, as in Great Britain, by the prospect of unemployment, poverty, and loss of initiative. Workers in this country received a larger share of the economic and social benefits of technological advance and as a result displayed less hostility. Only more recently has the attitude of labor to displacement by machinery aroused much public concern in the United States.

Objections to machinery were made and presented more calmly in the United States. For example, in 1784 Oliver Evans built an automatic flour mill near Philadelphia. The factory processes required no human labor from the time the grain was received at the mill until it emerged as flour packed in barrels at the end of the process. In 1813, millers called upon Congress for relief from the oppressive operations.[22] Substantial destruction of property appeared as random acts of vandalism, illustrated by the actions of the Molly Maguires in the anthracite coal industry during the middle of the nineteenth century, and the crude and spontaneous outbursts, demonstrated by the anarchistic International Working People's Association (Black International) in the 1880's. It was also used as a weapon of sabotage in the process of collective bargaining, as exemplified by the syndicalistic Industrial Workers of the World in the early part of the twentieth century. In these instances, the destruction was incidental to the matter of displacement of labor by machines.

The factory system of production did not become widely established in manufacturing in the United States until the

1880's when the introduction of machinery was widespread
and unprecedented in scope. Before 1870, skilled hand labor
was the basis of industry, and questions concerning the use
of machinery were not important in the American labor
movement. The only exceptions were in the production of
textiles, barrels, and shoes.

Machine production of textiles in the United States began
in the 1830's but did not involve competition with skilled
workers. Rather, it supplanted the work of women employed in the household. The first problem of displacement
of skilled workers by machines on a large scale occurred in
the shoe industry. Several inventions made it possible for
"green hands" to displace skilled workers in the production
of shoes. The meteoric rise and fall of the Knights of St.
Crispin during the decade beginning in 1867 resulted from
the refusal of employers to permit skilled workers to operate the shoe machines. The main object of this union was
to protect its members against the competition of unskilled
labor, and strike funds which the international accumulated
were intended to be used chiefly for this purpose. But starting in 1872 gradually increased and unified opposition by
employers to this union led to a disruption of the organization.

The introduction of machinery which led to new methods
of producing barrels was the direct cause of the formation
of a national union of coopers in 1870.[23] This organization,
however, could afford only minimal protection to the
workers.

Rapid mechanization in the 1880's enabled employers to
substitute unskilled workers, women, and children for the
skilled, but the equally rapid advance of production vastly
increased employment opportunities and minimized displacement effects. Labor shortages and high wages during
World War I opened another period of technological advance which reached a peak in the middle of the 1920's.
Displacement problems evoked much concern in labor,
management, governmental, and academic circles.

During the last decade of the nineteenth century there were several important attempts made by unions to stop the introduction of machinery, but these efforts were hardly more successful than the tactics of destroying machines had been earlier. The flint glass workers tried to prevent the use of semiautomatic bottle machines; the window glass workers opposed the use of sheet-drawing machines; and the stonecutters fought against the use of the stone planer. These union actions all failed in their purpose. The cigarmakers started with the same approach. There was resistance first to the bunch-breaking and roll-up system which introduced division of labor and lessened skill requirements and then to machine manufacture. But as these policies considerably weakened the union, they were abandoned in the mid-1920's.[24]

Nevertheless, a study of the relationship between the use of machinery and the employment of skilled labor concluded in the middle of the 1920's found that union policy had little effect on the amount of displacement which took place. Factors beyond the reach of union policy were more important.[25]

ECONOMIC THOUGHT AND LABOR-SAVING MACHINERY

Technological change which brings improvements and disruptions simultaneously to the economy has an impact both in the long-range and short-range periods. For a long time this impact has been an important factor in the development of civilization. Yet no satisfactory comprehensive and fully developed theory and analysis of the effects of technological change on employment and the role of such change in the economic process have been set forth. During the past century sporadic attention has been devoted to these matters by many persons. Aside from Karl Marx and, to a more limited extent, Joseph A. Schumpeter and Thorstein Veblen, however, the relationship between technological and economic change has not been explored by leading economists.

As a result of the perturbing problem of technological displacement of workers during the 1930's, a vast study of these many interrelated questions was undertaken by the United States Works Progress Administration, later called the Work Projects Administration. One aspect dealt with the theory of technological change. The study found that interest in the question of how much unemployment is caused by changes in technology had fluctuated widely during the two hundred years covering the period from the beginning of the Industrial Revolution to the present. It was also found that on each occasion when interest was renewed, the problem was considered to have unique or special characteristics. Although the presumption prevailed that overall gains derived by the community from technological progress far outweighed individual losses incurred, the public gradually came to recognize that the cost borne by those displaced was much too high.[26] Nevertheless, progress in alleviating distress during the decade of the 1930's was only slight and the expedients used were recognized as temporary.

Theoretical controversy in the literature of economics regarding the effects of technological change on employment was first introduced by the Mercantilists. "The attitude towards technical innovations, labour-saving machinery and the like, involved the mercantilists in . . . difficulties, and . . . led them into internal contradictions."[27] Similarly with the Physiocrats. Modern and more sophisticated analysis began with Adam Smith. It was he who set forth the ideas that the volume of production depends on the amount of capital and that technological advance (division of labor) is limited by the extent of the market. A more precise position is taken by Jean B. Say who, in the law of markets, maintains that dislocations in employment invariably are temporary and are automatically corrected because an increase in the supply of goods simultaneously increases demand for them. Two economists who did not agree with Say were Thomas R. Malthus and Simonde de Sismondi. They foresaw insufficiency of capital and lack of an adequate consumer market as conditions which could prolong unemployment brought about by technological advance.

David Ricardo at first thought that permanent displacement of labor by machinery was impossible, but after several years of reflection he concluded that a significant lag can develop in the demand for labor as investment in machinery continues to take place. Unlike Sismondi and Malthus, however, Ricardo conceived the adverse effects of machinery on labor to be a reduction in the production of consumer goods along with an increase in the amount of fixed capital rather than an overproduction of goods for consumption.[28] Ricardo's view, that increases in machinery might be disadvantageous to labor, was criticized by John R. McCulloch and Nassau W. Senior, both of whom reverted to the idea that workers displaced by machinery would be reabsorbed automatically. John Stuart Mill and John E. Cairnes amplified Ricardo's later position, formulating systematic theoretical notions of the possible unfavorable effects of technology on employment. Karl Marx also supported this view, but emphasized that the impact of machinery on employment is of a cyclical nature.

The attitude of workers and unions toward the advent of machinery was based only in part upon theory. As has been shown, almost from the beginning of the Industrial Revolution there is evidence of resistance by labor to the introduction of machinery which displaces workers. Though the fiercest opposition occurred in Great Britain, strong manifestations of displeasure were not lacking in France, the United States, and elsewhere. Factory machines of many kinds were destroyed. But this phenomenon was a temporary expedient which was abandoned under critical public pressure. It was replaced by restriction of output, more pervasive and sinister in character, a tactic through which workers sensed the ability to minimize the impact of technology.

Workers have justified the limitation of output on the basis of the "lump-of-labor" theory and "health-and-welfare" argument. The lump-of-labor argument, usually emphasized by craft workers, stresses that there is a fixed amount of work to be performed which is almost entirely independent of the cost of production or the price of the product. The number of labor units necessary to complete the task may be derived when the lump of work is divided by the amount of work which each individual performs. A greater number of labor units, resulting from lower individual output, could be used either to lengthen the working time of those already employed or to increase the number of workers.

Economists have generally denied the validity of this argument, but its relevance depends on time, place, and circumstances. During most of the nineteenth century, a similar type of relationship, the wages-fund doctrine—which assumed wages to be the quotient of the fixed wage fund and the number of workers—was a well-established principle in economic literature. To the extent that pure competition, mobility of labor, and the long-run period characterize the analysis, little justification for the lump-of-labor theory exists. But under conditions of a monopsonistic labor market, where frictions limiting the mobility of workers are great, and in a short-run period the notions of workers regarding work opportunities should not be lightly brushed aside. Workers are mainly concerned with their immediate standard of living rather than the future general welfare of society.

The health-and-welfare argument has been favored by the unskilled and industrial workers as an explanation for the need to regulate output. The ability to produce and the efficiency of the worker need to be considered in terms of his entire life span, and work beyond a certain pace impairs health and vigor. In order to conserve human resources a worker should expend no more energy than the amount which can be replaced by the food and rest he obtains.

Technological advance may be analyzed more appropriately in terms of production functions. A neutral technological advance, that is, one which is equally labor-saving and capital-saving, proportionately lowers the marginal cost of each factor used to produce a fixed volume of goods.

If demand for the product is elastic, the increase in volume of the good demanded will necessitate an increase in the amount of labor used. Thus, in a perfectly competitive economy if changes in technology require half the amount of each factor to be used to obtain the same output, the price will be cut in half. If demand is elastic, output will be more than doubled and the amount of labor employed will rise. When the demand for the product is inelastic, however, some loss of employment is indicated. Similarly, technological advance which is proportionately more capital-saving than labor-saving involves fewer labor displacement problems while changes which are proportionately more labor-saving than capital-saving cause more of them.

Actions by trade unions resisting the use of new or improved machinery and limiting output of industry were fully and convincingly described by the economist William T. Thornton 100 years ago.[29] He also clearly formulated the well-known lump-of-labor theory under which "at any given time the whole quantity of work to be done is a fixed quantity. . . ."[30] While recognizing the validity of this principle, he was nevertheless critical of many of the rules imposed by unions to increase the amount of work. These included provisions that stones must be worked by the masons at the place where they are used rather than at the quarry while they are soft; that the work of plasterers and other laborers must not be interchanged; that two men should be employed when one would be adequate; that building products used in any area must have been produced there; that bricks must be carried in a hod, no more than eight at a time, and should not be moved in wheelbarrows; that men should not walk beyond a given pace at work; that workers should not produce an amount which exceeds the output of the other employees; and that bricks made on one side of a canal should not be used for work being done on the other side.

John Stuart Mill felt that unions should use tactics other than restriction of output to protect their interests. He wrote:

There must be some better mode of sharing the fruits
of human productive power than by diminishing their
amount. . . . All restrictions on the employment of
machinery or on arrangements for economising labour,
deserve . . . censure. . . . I do not say that there are
never cases which justify a resort to measures even this
bad in principle. . . . But when thus acting, that portion of society is in a state of war with the rest. . . .
The true morality of the workmen would be to second
zealously all means by which labour can be economised
or made more efficient but to demand their share of the
benefit. In what shape they shall obtain it, is a matter
of negotiation between the parties, the difficulties of
which may be greatly lightened by an impartial arbitration.[31]

John E. Cairnes strongly disagreed with some of the ideas
expressed by Thornton.[32] He pointed out that people want
wages, not work; and that the rate of wages in any society
does not depend primarily on the quantity of work available.
Furthermore, Cairnes strongly objected to the notion that
the quantity of work to be done at any time is fixed. He
contended that it is indefinite and practically unlimited.
He admitted that technological change is almost always at-
tended by adverse effects on those displaced, but he maintained that these are temporary and transitory evils which
need to be alleviated by the community. In the longer
period, the gains made by labor from technology are great.
During the second half of the nineteenth century, the
importance of this question waned. The growth and expansion of the economies of the countries in the Western world
were marked by higher standards of living and increasing
volumes of employment. Alfred Marshall, John B. Clark,
and the other Neoclassical economists suggested that adjustments in the dislocation of labor caused by the introduction
of machinery are brought about automatically by operations
of the price mechanism. The matter of technological unemployment does not reappear in economic literature until
the 1920's. Reintroduction of the problem of technological

change and its effect on the demand for labor occurs in connection with an analysis of the business cycle, and its study is intensified as a result of the severe depression which began in 1929.[33]

GOVERNMENTAL INVESTIGATIONS

Controversies between management and labor became more intense in the United States during the last quarter of the nineteenth century. From time to time, labor strife, unrest, and violence were investigated by Congress and the executive branch of the federal government. Some of the reports issued as a consequence bear on the matters of technological displacement of labor and restriction of ouput.

In 1883, in the midst of efforts by labor to gain a firmer foothold in industry, an investigation was conducted by the United States Senate on the relations between labor and capital. It revealed the existence of a widespread belief among workers that too large a proportion of the benefits of labor-saving machinery are taken by the owners of industry. Fear of technological displacement was becoming evident. One witness testified to his impression that men generally believed inventions made during the preceding fifty years were doing nine-tenths of the work formerly done by manual labor in manufacturing. Another stated that industry had nearly exhausted the possibility of making further technological advance.[34]

As the tempo of technological advance increased in the United States, a joint Congressional resolution in 1894 directed the Commissioner of Labor to investigate and report upon some of the effects of the use of machinery on labor. A ponderous statistical study which compared hand and machine labor was completed in 1898. It said: "It is evident . . . that there has been a larger increase in the number of persons required for . . . production . . . in order to meet present demands, than would have been necessary to meet the limited demands under the hand-labor system." [35] The report contains no discussion of displacement, however.

The generally prevailing belief that union rules restricting the output of workers, which were far more common in Great Britain than in the United States, were responsible for the relative decline of British industry, led in part to two studies by the United States government at the beginning of the twentieth century of the attitude of labor toward industrial machinery and limitation of output. But the growth and mechanization of industry in the 1890's were of equal importance in stimulating investigations of displacement problems. It was clear that machines could adversely affect employees in two ways. First of all, machines could bring about the replacement of labor and reduction in the number of persons required to produce a given output and, secondly, they could curtail the amount of training and experience necessary to perform a job so that workers with lesser skills would be able to displace those with more.[36] The United States Industrial Commission was created by Congress in 1898 to make a broad survey and study of American industry; the United States Commissioner of Labor focused his entire attention on a comprehensive examination of the regulation and restriction of output.

The Industrial Commission made its final report in 1902. Its function in part was to investigate conditions of labor in the United States; and some of its findings concerned limitation of output and attitudes of labor organizations toward labor-saving improvements.[37] The Commission concluded that the reason why workers, whether organized or unorganized, resist labor-saving machinery arises because of the short-run effects. While the ultimate results of technological change upon the industry and the economy is usually beneficial, the immediate impact on the workers employed at the time is generally adverse. The Commission said: "It is . . . impossible to point out any instance in which unorganized workmen have received any immediate and visible benefit from the introduction of new machinery in their trade. Any number of instances might be pointed out in which they have suffered immediate and visible damage."[38] Other than checking technological progress, programs and plans which would reduce the hardships of the workers involved were desirable, according to the Commission. Certainly some of the benefits derived from introducing new machinery belong to the workers affected.

The first report devoted solely to the problems of restriction of output was published in 1904. Made by the Commissioner of Labor and prepared under the guidance of John R. Commons, it covers nearly all the industries in which restriction by employers or employees was alleged to exist at the time. In the report employers justified limitations on output because of the need to establish stable conditions, maintain fair profits and wages, and protect vested rights in machinery, equipment, patents, and copyrights. Employees and unions contended that restriction of output is necessary to protect skills of artisans, health, wages of workers, and quality of product. But some union emphasis was placed on making work, making the work go around, and retaliation against employers.

The report found that workers in the United States did not use retaliation as a weapon, though it was popular in Great Britain. Although union officials denied that workers engaged in making work or making work go around, "it is certain that this motive prevails widely among workmen themselves." [39] This motive was found more generally among older rather than younger workers. According to the report, makework policies were prevalent among nonunion wage earners, and restrictive practices were found to be strongly enforced in nonunion establishments. Union workers had not changed their nature; they had only acquired more power to carry out their demands.

During the first decade of the twentieth century, antiunion feeling was strong among employers. Representatives of employers on the United States Commission on Industrial Relations created by Congress in 1912 suggested in the final report than even a fair-minded employer might refuse to recognize and deal with unions because many of the labor organizations favor restriction of output.[40] This policy made it difficult for unionized employers to compete successfully

with nonunion shops. The commissioners cited testimony
by Louis D. Brandeis that the ideals of American democracy
can be attained only by greatly increasing the productivity
of men and that improvements in the conditions of workers
which marked the nineteenth and early twentieth centuries
resulted largely from the introduction of machinery and con-
comitant higher productivity of labor.[41] They stressed that
German industry far outpaced that of Great Britain because
British unions practiced restriction of output while German
workers did not.

The generally loose production standards maintained by
industry during World War I adversely affected productivity. A society of professional engineers headed by Herbert
Hoover set up a committee in 1921 to conduct a study of
the wastes in industry. Some of the findings dealt with the
role of labor. The study revealed considerable restriction of
output by labor because of fear of unemployment.[42] Unions
generally restricted, rather than prohibited, the use of machinery. Most of these practices were revealed to exist in
the building trades in connection with on site and hand
operations where shop and machine work were superior,
although wastes in several other industries were discussed.

The concern aroused in Congress by the heavy unemployment of the 1930's led to consideration of the effects of
technology. Members of Congress proposed measures requiring patent recipients of labor-saving machines to obtain
licenses before being permitted to use the devices and sus-
pending the issuance of patents for inventions which reduced
the use of labor. Several members of Congress felt that
taxes should be levied on the product of labor-saving equipment to discourage the displacement of workers. Prohibition of the use of labor-saving devices by federal agencies
was urged. None of these bills, however, was enacted.

In 1934 and again in 1935, several resolutions were introduced in the House of Representatives aimed at obtaining
data on displacement of workers by labor-saving devices
and requesting the Secretary of Labor to compile a list of
such machinery. In 1936, after hearings by a subcommittee

and recommendation by the committee on labor,[43] the House of Representatives passed a resolution directing the Secretary of Labor to list all the labor-saving devices designed to reduce the cost of production which had been put into operation since 1920 and to estimate the number of persons unemployed because of the use of these devices. The subcommittee said: "Your subcommittee . . . is of the opinion that mechanical and other labor-saving devices are the chief cause of the growing number of unemployed and prematurely superannuated derelicts among laborers. . . . If a laborer is unable to stand the strain [of speeding up], he is quickly replaced by a younger one waiting in line and begging for a job which will keep his body and soul together as long as that body will last in the grim, gruelling contest with a rapidly moving mechanical monster. . . ." [44] The subcommittee, supported by its chairman William P. Connery, Jr., recommended immediate passage of a thirty-hour week law as a "primary and logical" approach to the solution of the problem. One of the four members of the subcommittee which submitted this report was Congressman Fred A. Hartley, Jr., who was later to be a cosponsor of the Taft-Hartley Act, a law which exhibited vastly different sympathies in the opinion of the labor movement. The report was never submitted by the Secretary of Labor, because Congress did not provide sufficient funds to carry out the project. It is clear, however, that the projected undertaking was an enormous one that involved many practical difficulties and could not readily be presented in a meaningful way.[45]

Congressional interest in the displacement of labor by machinery continued throughout the 1930's. The subject was dropped from consideration as unemployment fell with the advent of the war in Europe. But the matter was revived in the late 1950's when persistent relatively high-level unemployment was ascribed in part at least to automation and technological change. As a result, Congress enacted legislation dealing with the problem.

Chapter II

THE CONCEPTS OF FEATHERBEDDING
AND SECURITY

Although resistance to technological advance and the restriction of output were used as techniques to safeguard jobs late in the nineteenth century in the United States, the full-fledged development of featherbedding with its many ramifications did not occur until the twentieth century was well under way. The likelihood of holding the same job through an entire working life became smaller. Strong unions sought ways to protect their members from the scourge of unemployment and technological displacement, and makework policies were adopted in many instances. Economic security has become one of the major goals of workers, unions, and the labor movement, but this orientation has raised questions as to whether economic growth, a factor necessary for higher standards of living, will be adversely affected. Thus far, economic theory has provided few answers to the complicated problems connected with featherbedding.

DEFINITION OF FEATHERBEDDING

The word "featherbedding" has been part of the English language for more than half a century but only recently has it been incorporated into the standard dictionaries.[1] Broadly speaking, it refers to practices or work rules which set unreasonable limits to the amount of work employees may do in a given period of time. It also includes payment for unneeded workers, unnecessary tasks, work not performed, or jobs duplicating those already done. More specifically and appropriately it means resistance by labor to the introduction of better techniques of production and more efficient types of machinery. The word, therefore, connotes contemptible behavior because it is associated with economic waste of resources and an unacceptable norm of conduct.

"Makework" is sometimes considered to be a broader category than featherbedding, although the words are often interchanged.[2] Unions ordinarily are interested in makework in industries where there exist declining or intermittent employment, unusually high wages and good working conditions, and the possibility that a large part of the membership will benefit from the policy. Fear of technological displacement, therefore, may not always be the cause of makework policies. There are many forms of makework. The types prevalent among a particular group of employees depend upon the technology and methods of production of the particular industry. A concise listing which includes most of the current practices shows six varieties of makework or featherbedding. These involve: limiting the work load an employee may handle or the number of machines he may operate; requiring unnecessary work or that work be done more than once; prohibiting certain labor-saving tools or machinery from being used; restricting the duties of workers or enforcing less efficient working methods and standards; requiring unnecessary standby workers or crews or an excessive number of workers; and compelling employers to grant excessive relief time. Some types of featherbedding, but not all, involve restriction of output.

The origin of the word "featherbedding" is not certain. One version of the origin of the word is that back in the 1850's soldiers of the United States frontier army who had easy jobs inside headquarters could sleep in comfortable featherbeds. They were called "featherbed soldiers."[3] A second account is that at the beginning of the twentieth century a group of employees of the Rock Island Railroad complained that their mattresses were filled with corncobs. The trainmaster said, "What do you want—featherbeds?"[4] Gradually the word grew to include many kinds of makework practices, and its use spread to other industries.

The objectives of the employer, which include greater profits, more efficiency, and—in most cases—increased output, form the main bases upon which work practices are judged to be featherbedding. But these economic values, which are not immutable, are not the only criteria considered in evaluating featherbedding practices. Employers have agreed to various conditions of work which may be in conflict with the goals of the firm, such as the elimination of sweatshops, the reduction in the daily hours of work to eight, an increase in the number of holidays, and extended vacations. Reliance on the judgment of management, however, is not always desirable. The existence of featherbedding is frequently identified by the objections of employers to certain practices rather than by the practices themselves. For example, the appropriate length of paid coffee breaks, call-in time, and wash-up time is a subjective decision which usually depends on the attitude of individual employers. As the debate over featherbedding has become more intense, the public has added other values for consideration in resolving the question of what should be done about makework, including economic security, dignity, and safety of the workers.

Work rules considered featherbedding sometimes are no more than an individual's desire for personal status or a conscious choice of leisure as an alternative to more output and higher wages. Secretary of Labor W. Willard Wirtz has said that featherbedding arises from a deep desire to work rather than from unwillingness to do so.[5] But the subject is complex and cases must generally be examined individually to be properly appraised. "The so-called featherbedding issue . . . involves thousands of highly particularized problems not amenable to understanding or treatment through broad generalization."[6]

Justification for union policies and actions which restrict output may be determined only by examining specific cases; condemnation is not merited by a general philosophy of life.[7] Typically, employees generally prefer to do an honest day's work rather than plan ways of reducing output. They also prefer to perform good work rather than poor. Dishonest performance not only ruins character but weakens collective bargaining by arousing hostility of employers to trade unionism.

There are three grounds upon which rules limiting the amount of work performed by labor are in order. These are health, safety, and reasonableness. It is universally recognized that labor is entitled to safe and healthful working conditions. The federal courts have upheld this proposition.[8] State laws afford many protections of this kind. The Labor Management Relations Act (Taft-Hartley Act) of 1947 indirectly deals with this matter. It specifies in Section 502 that employees who quit their jobs in good faith because of abnormally dangerous conditions of work at the place of employment are not considered to be on strike.[9] Overwork may be one such condition.

Work practices based on considerations of health and safety sometimes are confused with makework. The health or safety of an older worker may be endangered when working at a pace which is safe for a younger person. Rules setting the rate of output may be geared to the abilities of slower, but not necessarily incompetent, workers. In relatively few circumstances are work speeds reduced by unions simply to make jobs soft.

The classic illustration of makework, provided by Hans Christian Andersen's fairy tale "The Emperor's New Clothes" in which lazy swindlers are paid for weaving a nonexistent suit of clothes, reveals a type of action sometimes associated with workers or their unions. Employees negotiate work rules in collective bargaining as an alternative to other benefits and improvements in working conditions, or work rules may represent the specification of actual conditions prevailing at a particular time. In either case a rule may subsequently become obsolete, but workers feel they are entitled to a *quid pro quo* if it is given up.

Although it is difficult to establish the nature of reasonable effort, it is nonetheless necessary to do so. Otherwise, standards set by employers, which may be extreme, would have to be accepted as justified.[10] Limitations imposed by unions on decisions made by employers must, therefore, be examined carefully before being adjudged featherbedding and antisocial in character. Sometimes labor restricts output in order to maintain the quality of its work.

Factory production standards which determine a fair day's work are considered fair because they are so judged and accepted by those concerned, not because they are based on measurement. Work measurement serves as a tool for reaching agreement, not as a substitute for it. Ideas as to what constitutes a fair standard of work effort originate in the home or school and are modified at the place of work by experience, managerial attitudes which emphasize economic considerations, and social environment.

The idea of a fair day's work for a fair day's wage is not new. An agreement reached in 1900, though terminated in 1901, between the national metal trades association and the machinists specified that the union should "place no restrictions upon the management or production of the shop [but should] give a fair day's work for a fair day's wage."[11]

A fair day's work is another way of saying proper work load. Improvements in mechanical devices and equipment have led to many disagreements concerning proper work loads. More automatic machinery has made it possible for employers to assign a greater number of machines to the care of each worker, but this action has often brought charges by the union or from unorganized workers of stretch-out or unjustified increases in the amount of work demanded, particularly in the textile, hosiery, and garment industries. Disputes have arisen as to whether sufficient mechanical change had been made to warrant supervision of more machines by each operator or whether his health would be impaired by overwork under the new load. Union action has also been influenced, however, by the fact that the stretch-out has brought with it a certain amount of unemployment, at least in the short run.

It must be stressed that the concept of featherbedding is a function of time and place. For this reason, it is difficult to provide a definition which is invariably satisfactory. While it might be acceptable to state that an excessive number of workers constitutes one aspect of featherbedding, debate will be evoked when specific definition of "excessive" is attempted. Although it is likely that the gap between hours paid for and hours worked will continue to widen and, other things being equal, more men will be required to do the same amount of work, it does not follow that featherbedding will increase in these instances. This paradox comes about because the mores of our society have changed to meet the growing demand for leisure. The public and employers accept with almost no opposition the notion of shorter hours, longer vacations, more holidays, extended coffee breaks, and even occasional absence with pay for personal reasons in the construction of annual work schedules. Such working terms are typical of conditions in this country now. They reduce time on the job, yet are not considered to be featherbedding. But similar ideas evoked strong criticism in the United States a century ago and are frowned upon today in other parts of the world.

ECONOMIC SECURITY

Featherbedding practices almost invariably begin as efforts on the part of employees to protect their job security and employment opportunities. Employers normally oppose such tactics at first, but, recognizing the motive involved and fully realizing the immediate costs, they are willing to concede certain makework arrangements in exchange for withdrawal by workers of other demands. Generally, it is only at a later stage, when the practices have become firm and crystallized but the original fears that the workers had are no longer justified, applicable, or understood in the new situation that struggles by management to eliminate featherbedding occur. In the new context, the issue frequently revolves around stress by the unions on enforcing their work rules and by employers on exercising effective management rights.

An unemployed worker is unable to provide for himself and his family, and in addition he bears a rather unfavorable social stigma. Generally, the chief link between the worker and the world in which he lives is his job and the associations it makes possible and necessary. His work experience, skill, and income often provide the basis of status and authority not only among his fellow employees but also in his family and community life. Unemployment may be devastating and, especially if prolonged, could easily lead to the disintegration of an individual's relationship with those around him.

A wealthy society which provides a wide choice of consumer goods makes a worker more dependent on regular employment. "It may also have raised his personal stature and determination to keep what he's got and when this comes into conflict with the underlying fear of what redundancy can bring—even for a brief spell of unemployment—the result is tension in industrial relations." [12]

Featherbedding ordinarily consists of union policies and rules designed to resist introduction of new machinery, to create an excessive number of jobs, and to require unnecessary work to be performed. It may be specified in labor agreements, included in union bylaws and manuals, or observed in customary performance. But restriction of output is not necessarily a policy determined by unions and imposed on their members. Studies have shown that nonunion workers develop standards of appropriate work loads which they impose through social pressure on newly hired employees.

Featherbedding practices have various counterparts in economic behavior. Many institutional arrangements which restrict output or productivity are not subject to public criticism, or are only mildly so. These include the suppression of patents by large manufacturers intent on preserving the value of invested capital, achievement of economic monopoly and gaining the attendant unearned or monopoly profits by restricting output, limitation on the output of crops which farmers practice under the guidance of agencies of the federal government, and reduction in consumer demand effected by price-fixing under fair trade legislation enacted for the benefit of small retailers. These actions are all designed to advance the economic interests of producers of goods and services at the expense of the users. Public criticism is usually greater when workers resist technological advance than when employers restrict output because the latter use logic which is more readily rationalized and techniques which are subtler.

Reduction in output below a level attainable without undue effort is ascribable to several factors. Workers might be lazy and try to minimize the amount of work they perform. This type of behavior must be condemned. Sometimes employees expect to prevent a reduction in incentive rates by keeping output down. Even if increases in output result solely from the ingenuity of the workers, management is normally forced to adjust wage rates downward in order to prevent the development of a chaotic wage structure and grave inequities in wages paid for similar jobs. Occasionally, however, the alleged basis of a reduced work pace is to protect the health and safety of workers. In these instances great care must be taken in evaluating the effects of work.

Most frequently, and here lies the crux of the problem, the worker is obsessed by profound fears of unemployment and will use any device or strategy to prolong the duration of a job he expects will soon end. It is in connection, therefore, with declining industries, casual or intermittent types of employment, and technological advance that workers are likely to resist most strongly the attempts by employers to eliminate or modify rules which tend to reduce the amount of work each man does. The failure of makework where markets are shifting or industries declining is inevitable. Even if demand is inelastic, attempts to mitigate unemployment by imposing work restrictions can only bring temporary relief in these cases. Rising labor costs only accelerate factor and product substitution. Industries such as construction and longshoring and activities performed by musicians and actors which provide casual employment do not solve their problems by enlarging the labor force they attract. The usual consequence is a lower average income for the workers involved. Attrition and retraining are the two main forces which must be relied upon to minimize the adverse effects of declining work opportunities.

Industrial workers are faced by insecurity of employment and scarcity of jobs because frequently there are more employees attached to an industry than can be provided with steady work. Several reasons are present for this condition. Some industries are undergoing secular declines; others are subject to great cyclical fluctuations in output. Some industries are faced with recurring seasonal influences of great magnitude, and a few, for a variety of reasons, offer only intermittent employment opportunities. Unions have attempted to deal with these situations in a number of ways. Restricting the supply of labor is common. Principles of seniority and sharing the work have been in effect for long periods of time. Guaranteed hours of work and guaranteed wages are other devices used. But unions have also tried to maintain or add to the amount of work available by increasing the demand for labor. Campaigns to increase the sale of the product are usually undertaken by unions in conjunction with employers. Some of the efforts made to increase the demand for labor constitute featherbedding.

Even more so than in the past, society is caught in the meshes of the dilemma posed by the alternatives of individual freedom and financial security. To a large extent, the problem arises only in an industrial environment, when workers live in cities and become dependent upon factory wages for a livelihood. Under the domestic system, they were often able to fall back on the generosity of nature which made provision for minimum subsistence from the food and fiber products yielded by the small plot of land they cultivated. Increased insecurity, however, is offset by some economic advantages. Living standards ordinarily rise for those city dwellers who are employed.

During the nineteenth century, when capitalism was making rapid strides, the Western world became more enamored of democracy as a way of life. The major characteristics which identified the institution of democracy were the existence of political liberty and the protection of life and property by the government. But greater outputs and expanding economies brought with them misery for much of the labor force. Women and children were exploited mercilessly, and men were subject to the vicissitudes of recurrent unemployment. Gradually, under these conditions, the concept of democracy changed for many persons. It developed into the notion that the major criterion of the existence of democracy was the prevalence of economic security. Undue disparity of income had to be eliminated and equality of economic opportunity assured and protected.[13] The emphasis which previously had been placed on rugged individualism and the right of persons to remain free from all but very limited governmental interferences and encroachments gave way. The new ideas of democratic living stressed the importance of job security.

John R. Commons traced the concept of labor as a form of property belonging to the laborer back to Adam Smith; he concluded that workers own an expectancy dependent upon the goodwill of employers but do not own the jobs they are hired to perform.[14] In his cogent analysis of the labor movement, Selig Perlman reasoned that unions seek to control the limited number of job opportunities in order to function effectively. One objective of unions is to become the virtual owner and administrator of the available jobs. If this is not possible, unions try through collective bargaining to establish rights in jobs for the individual and the group by negotiating rules concerning seniority, overtime, apprenticeship, and the introduction of machinery.[15]

The idea that workers possess property rights in their jobs developed slowly, but was clearly expressed as early as 1920. One statement of the principle was that "the trade unionist invokes the patrimonial rights of the worker in his particular trade and particular job. Consequently . . . innovations in the processes of production and introduction of machinery, which disturbs the 'established expectation' of the worker with respect to wages and conditions of employment is conceived to be a violation of the vested rights of the workers." [16] Some others studying labor conditions were of a similar opinion.[17]

A rather precise exposition of the concept of property and vested rights in the job was made in 1937 by Dean Leon Green of Northwestern University Law School in connection with the activities of the sitdown strikers. He wrote that both employers and employees ". . . have contributed heavily to the joint enterprise of industry. The contributions of those who make up the corporate organization on the one hand are visualized in plant, machinery, raw materials and the like. They can be seen, recorded and valued in dollars. We call them property. On the other side are hundreds of personalities who have spent years training their hands and senses to specialized skills; who have set up habitations conveniently located to their work; who have become obligated to families and for facilities necessary for maintaining them; who have ordered their lives and developed disciplines; all to the end that the properties essential to industry may be operated for the profit of the owner group and for their own livelihoods. Their outlays are not so visible, nor so easily measured in dollars, but in gross they may equal or even exceed the contributions of the other group. Both groups are joint adventurers, as it were, in industrial enterprise. Both have and necessarily must have a voice in the matters of common concern. Both must have protection adequate to their interests as against the world at large as well as against the undue demands of each other." [18]

The claim that a worker has on a job he holds has not been fully developed nor widely recognized. It is more generally accepted that a person is entitled to have an opportunity to make a living than that employers or the government owe him a living. But sometimes it is suggested that when workers are deprived of jobs they give up property and should, therefore, be entitled to compensation.[19]

Work rules, which very often are obtained by workers only at the cost of taking smaller increases in wages and other benefits, have tended to establish certain rights of workers in connection with their jobs. They have sometimes involved resolution of a conflict between a fair day's work and the health and safety of employees. Supreme Court Justice Arthur J. Goldberg, when counsel for the CIO, suggested that working rules are an attempt to find a "middle ground between workers being worked too hard and workers lying down on the job." He stated that the stretch-out or speed-up is the employer's version of featherbedding—performance of additional work without more pay in contrast to demands for additional pay without more work.[20] Work rules give employees some measure of protection, and it may well be that they provide that degree of security which enables workers to concentrate on their jobs rather than on the unsteadiness of employment and to thereby increase output.

During the past fifteen years the struggle by unions to establish the right of workers to a job has led to the inclusion of clauses in collective bargaining contracts dealing with plant removal and relocation. Formerly, a union tried to secure job protection for its members through apprenticeship regulations. But as unionism expanded to include many workers outside crafts, more emphasis has been put on seniority. It is sometimes recognized that vested or property rights, which accrue to employees who have seniority, survive the contract that created the rights. Consultation with the union, continuation of the contract at the new site, or job offers to the employees may be required before the employer is permitted to transfer his plant. Decisions by arbitrators and state and federal courts have not been consistent thus far on the rights and obligations of the parties. One federal circuit court held that seniority gives workers vested rights in jobs, and they are entitled to employment

in the new establishment if a plant relocates.[21] Another
federal circuit court, however, decided that seniority does
not give any vested rights to employees.[22]

The developments relating to job security opened up questions concerning conflict between the interests of society at
large and its constituent members. It is clear that gains may
be made by the group as a whole while individuals are
undergoing hardship. The economic progress of society
does not mean that *every* person benefits or even that most
of them do so at all times.

ECONOMIC GROWTH

The relationship between economic security and economic
progress is a complex one. Growth of the economy implies
changes in methods and ideas. Economic growth is not only
brought about by change; it also causes change. Working
habits and skills cannot remain unaltered in an economy
which is expanding. Slow and gradual adjustments which
reduce the need for men to shift geographically or occupationally also curb the processes of growth. Planning is not
always possible or feasible when it involves predicting the
course of technological advance or shifts in consumer
demand.

The link between featherbedding and economic growth
extends beyond the number of man-hours available for
productive effort. Employee morale is an important factor
in determining output and productivity, even if it cannot be
readily quantified.

Restrictive rules which generally accompany makework
and featherbedding are intended to limit or bar changes in
the operations of industry. The processes involved in growth,
however, are rarely smooth. They require experimentation
with new methods of production or alteration in those
already firmly established. The greater the freedom, the
more likely the prospects for substantial success. Gradual
and smooth transition is less conducive to economic growth.
Regulating or controlling changes tend to misallocate or

squander resources because of the difficulty of anticipating production problems or predicting the demand of consumers.

Economic growth is important not only as a means of raising the standard of living and meeting the challenges of foreign countries and other economies in a turbulent world but as the major source of new and more jobs. In the longer period, it is only through the elimination of restrictions on output rather than by encouraging makework that additional work opportunities will be created.

Nevertheless, society has come more and more to recognize the importance of human values. It is no longer the costs of machinery alone which determine the desirability of industrial projects and undertakings. Efforts to increase growth and productivity now take account of the impact which changes have on the lives of people.

Complete economic security requires stability, and the inherent conflict between growth and stability requires a choice. Featherbedding is a device to increase security, but it can be utilized only if the nation is willing to accept a slower rate of growth. It is at this point that a fundamental determination must be made respecting the degree of economic security which society wishes to guarantee the individual, recognizing that security may be increased only at the cost of reducing the potential output. At best, however, the goal of security is elusive. Walter P. Reuther has said that workers are engaged in a common though false "search for security in an insecure world." [23]

John K. Galbraith disagrees with this view. He points out that though insecurity is considered an underlying basis of the competitive system, it is gradually being eliminated in the real world. Since persons who have something to protect are the ones who seek security, businessmen were the first to attempt to safeguard their property and businesses from the effects of competition; in a large measure they have been successful. Economic security has only recently become important to ordinary workers—as real wages have risen and well-being has increased. For Galbraith there is no inconsistency between the increase of production and the mitigation of insecurity. A high level of production is necessary for a high degree of security and vice versa.²⁴ But Galbraith does not make out a strong case for his contentions. As he himself states, economists generally have not shared this view.

Valid economic objection to featherbedding must be based to a large extent on the undesirable effects which these practices have on economic growth. If two men work on a job which one should do, featherbedding is reducing the effectiveness of the labor force and preventing the gross national product from reaching its full potential. It is advantageous to the long-run growth of the economy if employers increase wage outlays to those they are already employing rather than make payments to additional employees hired in connection with restrictive practices which arrest technological advance even if the immediate cost and output in both cases are the same. Restrictive practices curtail output, but increased expenditures on higher wages might only tend to cause inflation. The growth of the economy is also affected adversely if payment is made when work is not performed, since these funds could be used by employers for productive effort, including capital formation.

Criticism of featherbedding should not arise simply because the costs of operating a business are higher. If the workers are strong enough they will raise wages so that they replace the income lost when the amount of makework is reduced. Thus the elimination of bogus typesetting would tend to bring about higher wages, and the total labor costs of the printing industry would remain the same. No benefits to the economy would result unless additional manpower became available for productive effort. To the extent, however, that bogus work is performed by printers during slack hours of employment and no alternative duties would be imposed, economic effects are not significant.

If the advantages of economic growth are to be derived from the elimination of featherbedding, there is an underlying assumption that the saving in manpower utilization will not be dissipated by a reduction in hours. But pressure to absorb those separated from jobs might lead to curtailment in the standard work week and adversely affect growth in an economy of full employment, even though it beneficially increases the average amount of leisure time. There are numerous implications stemming from an increase in leisure, an important one being the shift of productive resources to service industries, particularly those concerned with recreation and entertainment. Whether increased free time for workers would lead to a larger volume of growth, because of either the greater vigor and vitality made possible by more relaxation or as a consequence of a stimulus to demand which could develop, is highly problematical. But it is certainly necessary in any event to pay close attention to the actual working time of the labor force if one of the main concerns is to increase the output of the economy.

Another economic argument against featherbedding relates to the misallocation of resources. An industry burdened by higher costs and, therefore, higher prices is at a disadvantage when there are substitutes for its products or services, the disadvantage being greater when demand is more elastic. For example, the alternative means of freight transport, particularly trucking, make the railroads quite vulnerable to the impact of higher costs brought on by featherbedding. If a substantial saving in labor costs could be effected by eliminating men whose performance plays no essential part in the operation of the industry and if the competitive disadvantage of the industry could be reduced, part of the market might be recaptured by the railroads. The benefits of a competitive economy would then be available to those who ship goods. But beyond this public gain, investors in the industry entitled to a return on their capital would have a fairer opportunity of deriving such payments.

CONTRIBUTIONS OF ECONOMIC THEORY

The political, social, human, and legal considerations involved in featherbedding are of such magnitude that pure

economic analysis affords very little prospect of providing a
solution. Simple and intricate models of union behavior
serve little purpose in resolving questions in which other
considerations are paramount. Furthermore, Slichter has
remarked that analysis of makework practices in static terms
by using the notions of elasticity of demand and elasticity
of substitution "is not worthwhile," because the principal
effect of limitations on output is to cause employers to search
even more zealously for ways and opportunities to alter
technology.[25] Yet a description of the subject in a rigid
economic framework helps to pinpoint and clarify some of
the concepts and to diagnose some of the problems.

Unions have several economic alternatives. Simply stated,
they may demand higher wages for a given amount of employment, more employment at a particular wage, or increases in both wages and employment. Featherbedding is
involved if unions demand higher wages for a specified
number of employees explicitly or implicitly set above
equilibrium, more employment than the equilibrium amount
determined by the market wage, or influence on the production function through a voice in determining how to use
the firm's employees or how many additional workers are
to be hired.

Each of the various types of featherbedding, whether involving the complete elimination of effort by workers (as
in the case of standbys who receive specified hourly payments), the reduction in the effort expended by workers,
or the maintenance of the normal intensity of effort in the
performance of work which is not essential or necessary to
production, causes a decline in the number of units of
effective labor effort (as distinguished from the number of
man-hours or workers) offered at any given wage or an
increase in the wage rate necessary to bring forth a specified
number of units of effective labor effort. The effect on the
size of the payroll, however, depends on the elasticity of
demand. If demand for labor is inelastic, then the payroll
increases as a result of featherbedding. The number of man-
hours of labor hired or employment also increases. On the

other hand, if the demand is elastic then both the payroll and employment decline.

Of course, similar conclusions are reached if the analysis is made in terms of the product of labor. When employers are forced to use more labor per unit of output, unit cost of production rises. It follows that the commodity will tend to rise in price and the volume of sales will fall. The elasticity of demand for the product will determine whether the increased employment effects brought about by featherbedding exceed the decreased employment effects resulting from a reduced output. The overall extent of featherbedding in the economy at any time may cause indirect employment effects, depending on whether overtime is used or additional workers are hired, and income effects, depending on changes in total payrolls.

Workers normally consider the demand for labor to be inelastic and under such conditions pressures to make work are expected to increase the quantity of labor hired. In the short run this attitude is realistic in most situations. It is in the longer period, where demand for labor becomes more elastic as factor and product substitutions are made, that the impact on employment is unfavorable. Since it takes some time for an adverse effect on employment to occur, workers are not always inclined to associate the effect with the cause in the longer run. Rather, they attribute unemployment to factors other than featherbedding.

In a static economy, unless monopoly profits are available, demands for increases in wages or man-hours cannot be met beyond the short run, because they lead to business losses and failures. But typically, workers are successful in raising wages or increasing employment because the derived demand for labor increases as the economy grows and demand for the product rises. The ability of employers to absorb additional hours without decreasing wages or to raise wages without reducing man-hours depends upon the degree of elasticity of demand for labor. Wage or man-hour increases granted by employers often anticipate growth in the economy or rising productivity.

The elimination of featherbedding practices is difficult where technological advance brings on a contraction in the demand for labor while the union attempts to maintain man-hours and wages. In such cases an industry which has no monopoly profits can operate successfully without reducing hours only if it cuts wages or undertakes an equivalent, that is, it reduces fringe benefits or safety standards. If the decline in demand for labor is short run, the problem can ultimately be worked out. If, however, the industry is declining or the market is shifting, an alternative to displacement may not be found. Under these circumstances, a union may obtain temporary respite from unemployment for its members by imposing makework on an employer, provided his demand for labor is inelastic. The employment situation is only aggravated if demand is elastic. But even in the former case, over a period of time, adjustments and changes in operations by employers will increase the elasticity of demand for labor.

Chapter III

THE STATUS OF FEATHERBEDDING

Featherbedding and makework have become deeply embedded in the economy as a result of the long exposure by industry to these practices. There always has been criticism of the wastes engendered by featherbedding, and currently such views are relatively strong. The ultimate disposition of the practices involved depends largely on the attitudes of the different groups which will help determine public policy. Nevertheless, it is clear that featherbedding instituted through union rules does not pervade the entire economy. Rather, it is limited to a relatively small number of industries and occupations. The cost of featherbedding is a burden which is unnecessary, since other means of providing more job security must be made available, but the exact amount of the burden is difficult to ascertain.

PREVALENT ATTITUDES

Employers, employees, unions, government, and the public have participated in the controversy and debate regarding makework activities. While most efforts and practices which lead to restriction of output are universally condemned, each group condones some actions under particular circumstances. Furthermore, the attitudes and policies toward featherbedding have not always been consistent and frequently have not been clear cut.

The most important factor bearing on attitude and policy is the financial position of the firm and the state of prosperity of the economy. Activities which are ignored when

51

conditions are favorable become burdensome and intolerable when the economic climate is adverse.

Employers

Employers more than any other group object to featherbedding. Since they most readily perceive the costs involved in makework and recognize that profits will rise if savings are effected, their opposition is not surprising. The issue of makework is a good one for employers to stress because the American people have shown little sympathy for restriction of output. For this reason unions have been hard-pressed to defend such practices. But the attitude of management does vary; it shows more resistance when business conditions are unfavorable.

Labor frequently counters charges by employers, claiming that management itself is guilty of much featherbedding in its own ranks. The American Institute of Management, an organization sponsored by industry, disclosed that considerable makework exists in the United States at the highest levels of management. Nepotism, which may be considered a form of featherbedding, was found in almost 12,000 of the 23,000 companies studied.[1] There was a complete absence of management featherbedding in less than ten per cent of companies examined.[2] Such conditions prevailed not only in business firms, but also in trade associations and non-profit foundations.

The causes of featherbedding at the executive level include greed, insecurity, inadequacy, and misplaced loyalties. Nepotism generally has been an important factor. Mergers sometimes bring to a firm an excessive number of executives. Incompetents occasionally are promoted to reduce their influence on production policies of the company. Long-term employment contracts received by some high executives are not always warranted. In some cases, executives surround themselves with agreeable rather than efficient assistants. The Institute concluded that " . . . in management featherbedding the damage is greater, the cost is larger and the bad example set is far more obvious."[3]

Nonunion Workers

Although featherbedding is usually discussed in connection with trade unionism, it has always been clear that unorganized workers are just as prone to engage in restriction of output. Workers in industrial society, regardless of whether or not they are organized, oppose the introduction of new industrial machinery because it arouses the fear of unemployment. The reaction has varied, however, depending on the state of unionization. Nonunion workers have been more inclined to reach tacit understandings and bring social pressures on the members of the work group. These actions are more difficult to isolate and identify than formal rules and contractual provisions.

The United States Industrial Commission stated quite definitely in 1902 that unorganized workers were responsible for restriction of output. It found that unions are necessary to establish and institute rules limiting output, but the unions only concretize tendencies and desires already in existence. Rules of this nature generally are expressions of trade traditions.[4] Though the report by the Commissioner of Labor in 1904 was concerned mainly with restriction of output by unions, several illustrations of similar action by nonunionists are given.[5]

John Mitchell, the youthful president of the coal miners' union, pointed out in 1903 that unorganized workers as well as those who are unionized restrict output.[6] Max Weber, the eminent German sociologist, noted in 1908 that conscious and intentional restriction of output is found not only among the organized, but among nonunion workers who share a feeling of solidarity.[7] Twelve years later the psychologist Charles S. Myers agreed that nonunionists engage in restriction of output.[8] The most exhaustive and systematic study of restriction of output among unorganized workers was completed by Mathewson in 1930. This investigation was concerned with a very large number of specific instances of limitation of output by nonunion workers and concluded that the practice is sufficiently prevalent

"to constitute a major problem in American industry." The
investigation raised, but left unanswered, the question of
whether unorganized workers are responsible for more restriction than union labor.[9] Findings by the International
Labour Office in 1954, that the roots of restrictive practices
lie deep in human nature and have long antedated the
unionization of workers, were anticlimactic.[10] Group pressures normally set the work pattern and objections from
management have been few.

Unionized Workers

The attitude of unionized workers toward technological
progress which has led to the imposition of restrictive practices stems from various factors. These include the attitude
and behavior of management, the satisfaction of employees
with working conditions, the size and type of union, and the
history of the union and its relations with other labor organizations. Most important of all, workers are influenced by
employment conditions in the labor market. Nevertheless,
there has been a gradual realization by workers that a
proper distribution of the costs and gains of new technology
is the key to improvement of conditions, and as a result
resistance to technological progress generally has been
abandoned. Gains are represented by advances in the standard of living and more leisure time; costs include the loss
of skills and experience, the need for some displaced workers
to find new jobs and shift their places of residence, and the
inability of other employees to readjust.

Evolution in the attitude and behavior of workers toward
the introduction of new machines has depended in great
part on surrounding circumstances. The most serious cases
of resistance to machinery and the clearest demonstrations
of destructive human impulses and mob violence occurred
at those times and places in which workers affected by the
installation were faced by a variety of restrictions limiting
their ability to change trades or move to other locales.
Geographical and job mobility formerly were subject to

legal restraints and limited by the practicalities of life. It is for this reason that the greatest difficulties of adaptation to new machinery occurred in Great Britain at the end of the eighteenth and beginning of the nineteenth century. Employees in that environment saw no reemployment prospects when machines put them out of work. Resistance lessened somewhat in England as workers became more mobile. In the United States, where laborers have almost always had greater freedom to move about, physical destruction of machines intended to displace humans was much rarer. The last half of the nineteenth century and first part of the twentieth, years when restrictions on the movement of workers were minimal, saw the smoothest industrial transition to labor-saving machinery. More recently, the greater impact of severe economic depressions, the accumulation of rights and privileges under the systems of seniority, and the existence of vested interests in pension funds have made it far less attractive for workers to seek new jobs or change their places of residence. Resistance to technological advance, although expressed in much milder forms than formerly, has again become an important industrial issue.

Unions

As already indicated, the question of whether trade unions limit output became important in the United States near the beginning of the twentieth century. At first, discussion did not revolve around the impact of technology on the attitudes and activities of workers. The main concern was whether the amount of work assigned was overly burdensome and unduly sapped the physical vitality and stamina of workers, thereby making them useless to industry in relatively short periods of time. Generally, it was not contended that union leaders exerted pressure on workers to reduce the normal amount of work performed during working hours. Rather, the labor movement was interested in achieving a reduction in the daily hours of work, an objective more widely acceptable outside the wage-earning class.

At times employers agreed to permit their workers to produce less in lieu of giving them an increase in wages; occasionally and possibly for brief intervals strong locals reduced work loads of their members below reasonable limits.[11] There are instances where unions, such as stove mounters, flint glass workers, and iron and steel workers, have tried to avoid a cut in the piece rate paid to their members by limiting the amount of wages which workers were allowed to earn in a day.

Trade unions generally favored policies limiting output only to resist the speed-up. It sometimes happened that employers hired several very able workmen who were induced by financial arrangements to set a work pace above the normal capabilities of most workers in order to drive those on the job to greater exertion. It was not unusual near the turn of the century, according to reports, for the rapidity of the pace of work to cause the mental exhaustion and physical collapse of workers.[12] Furthermore, union policy required that no man should undercut the wage set by collective bargaining. Yet one worker could underbid another just as easily by offering more work for the same wage rate. These situations imposed upon trade unions the necessity of fighting to regulate output. But as the practice of the speed-up was gradually abandoned by employers, limitation of output as a union countermeasure became less important.

Some union opposition to new machinery resulted from unhappy experiences. Technological advance made it easier for employers to institute the speed-up, destroyed skills, reduced the demand for labor in establishments using new devices, and sometimes made possible the employment of women and children. But even at the beginning of the twentieth century, attempts by unions to prevent the use of machines were comparatively few. Rather, they tried to exercise that degree of control which would permit their members to operate the machines at wages at least as high as those formerly prevailing. The typographers succeeded in this objective. Other regulations were devised. Machinists, pressmen, and lithographers, for example, fixed the number of machines each man could operate.

But the bakers' union, predominantly craft in nature, which had incomplete control of the labor market, did not show hostility to technological advance. This union did, however, generally press harder for shorter hours in the mechanized sector of the industry. As machines replaced hand labor, the organization assumed more of the characteristics of an industrial union. The advantages which workers receive from mechanization have been recognized by the union leadership. In 1955, the president of the bakers' union said: "We have 170,000 members in the union . . . but I doubt if 16,000 of them are bakers. . . . But the machines, while eliminating bakers, require great numbers of men to assemble the packaging materials, store and move the products. We've exchanged bakers for bakery workers." [13]

In one sector of the labor market, however, where control was complete, the bakers' union resisted technology and practiced featherbedding. In 1922, the New York State Joint Legislative Committee on Housing (the Lockwood Committee) conducted an investigation of the Jewish bakers union in New York City. It disclosed, among other things, that: union policy required the hours of work were to be reduced if machinery is used in a bakery; employers were to limit the amount of bread baked each day; during specified periods an employer "must keep and pay such number of men as the union determines even if he has no work for so many"; and bakery machinery was to be operated by journeymen workers only. The committee found that these rules drove employers out of business because they were unable to compete with the city's non-Jewish bakers who were not burdened by similar requirements. [14]

There are instances in which unions whose members are affected by technological change are not always capable of acting effectively. This occurs, for example, when new developments or growth in one industry influence employment opportunities in another. In some situations, alterations in the techniques of production are minor and do not arouse the interest of the union. Union policy toward technological change takes the form of opposition and competition, acceptance and encouragement, or adjustment and control. In general, unions have not been able to prevent technological advance by opposition, except temporarily or locally. Indeed, restrictions and high wage demands have sometimes induced change. The tendency has been for unions to adjust to change and seek to control it under policies which assume that high wages and low labor costs should be achieved simultaneously. The fruitlessness of resistance historically has been amply demonstrated. The growth of industrial unionism and the broadening of craft union jurisdiction have influenced union outlook. The labor movement, recognizing the inevitability of change and the futility of resistance, curbs its impulses.

Attempts by the union to exert control over employment opportunities when technological displacement occurs have been hampered by jurisdictional disputes over work, particularly among craft unions. These controversies have made it difficult for any one union to work out an agreement with employers regarding job control. The situation has been further aggravated in some instances when technological advance has changed the nature of the tasks, because the narrow basis of craft unionism has limited the scope of duties which workers are expected to perform. Furthermore, as a matter of policy employers have sometimes resisted union claims for jurisdiction of new types of work evolving from technological change.

But labor has recognized that it must extend its jurisdiction over new machines, jobs, and processes when they are introduced if it is to prevent the contraction of union membership or the extinction of unions. Prohibiting its members from operating new equipment has almost always proved harmful to the union and unsuccessful in providing security for the membership. Such has been the experience of the molders, window glass workers, stonecutters, and cigarmakers.

Union efforts to increase the degree of employment security enjoyed by workers have been supported in part by those employers who believe that insecure workers are prone to be less efficient. In trying to control and adapt to technological change, unions have sought to protect employment opportunities, earnings, and the conditions of work of their members. Although these efforts are similar to those which unions make in connection with all collective bargaining negotiations for the improvement of working conditions, the policies dealing with machine displacement have a number of unique characteristics. Minimizing displacement includes union concern with factors relating to limitations on work loads, transfer to other jobs, retraining, regulating the rate at which machines are introduced, controlling the number of new entrants to the trade, reduction in hours, and maintenance of earnings. Unions may also try to attain greater security and job tenure for members through seniority arrangements and work guarantees. Determination of the work load deals mainly with the intensity of labor and has often been linked by unions to the health of workers and the safety of operations. In actuality, however, it sometimes involved maintenance of employment in the form of featherbedding. The other goals represent more legitimate attempts to alleviate distress brought on by technological advance.

The authors of a thorough study of makework practices concluded that the effects of union policies in controlling the introduction of new machines tend to distort the wage structure in a plant because relatively higher wages are paid to those workers assigned to the new machines or processes; to cause employers using the new techniques to hire excessive crews under makework rules; and to reduce the adverse displacement impact on workers through more gradual introduction of changes.[15]

Labor Leadership

Except for the decade of the 1930's, the leadership of the American labor movement has remained firm against restriction of output and resistance to technological advance. John

Mitchell, president of the coal miners' union, wrote at the turn of the twentieth century that production difficulties arise from the attitude of employers that workers should be paid as little as possible for the maximum amount of work, and the responding reaction of employees to offer as little work as possible for the highest wage that can be obtained. But he added that policies of American unions generally are not restrictive; he stated: "The slogan of trade unionists should be, and is, a fair day's work for a fair day's wage . . ." [16] Generally, heads of national unions have usually expressed themselves in the same vein.

Samuel Gompers plainly indicated on numerous occasions that the labor movement must not struggle against technological advance. In his autobiography he relates that he learned the futility of opposing technological progress about 1869 when the cigarmakers' union, of which he was a member, lost a hard-fought strike against the introduction of molds and bunch-breaking machines in the industry.[17] In 1919 Gompers wrote: "The working people of the United States, have never considered, much less adopted, a policy of limitation of output, and in the last twenty years not even has any appreciable group of workers followed any such policy. It is . . . foreign to the whole code of ethics of the organized labor movement." [18] Ten years later, William Green, Gompers' successor as president of the AFL, said: " . . . the American labor movement welcomes the installation and extension of the use of machinery in industry." [19] In the 1930's the AFL contended that the principal cause of unemployment was technological displacement, and that Congressional investigations to study the problem should be held so that actions to reduce distress might be taken. John L. Lewis and Philip Murray, the first and second presidents of the CIO, felt that employers should be free to introduce new machinery.[20] George Meany, currently president of the AFL-CIO, has said that the labor movement recognizes the advantages of automation and does not want to stop progress; it wants only to minimize social and economic dislocations.[21]

The Public

Public feeling toward featherbedding is mainly intuitive. In principle, anathema and revulsion for such practices seem morally correct. Yet in specific instances, especially when personal interests appear to be at stake, less critical reaction has been manifest. Attempts to measure public reaction to featherbedding have been undertaken on a number of occasions by the American Institute of Public Opinion (Gallup Poll) over the past quarter of a century.[22]

Generally, surveys have posed the following question to the general public and to persons who are members of families with one or more union members: "In order to provide work for union members, some unions require more workers than are actually needed on a job. How do you feel about this—should there be a law against this practice or not?" The first poll, in July, 1943, revealed that sixty-nine percent of the public felt there should be legislation, nineteen percent felt there should not be, and twelve percent had no opinion. Subsequent tabulations, as the public has come to understand the problems better and as the labor market has loosened, have shown a considerable lessening of hostility. In 1944, sixty-two percent favored a law and seventeen percent were opposed; in 1945, the distribution was sixty-six percent and twenty percent; in 1946, it was sixty percent and twenty-three percent;[23] and in 1959, it was fifty-four percent and twenty-six percent. The most recent survey, taken in April, 1962, showed fifty-five percent of the public in favor of legislation and twenty-three percent opposed.[24] Among persons in families with union members, those favoring legislation have always been a smaller fraction of the group than in the public at large. In this group, about half of those surveyed (with a downward trend) have favored legal prohibition of makework and a third have opposed such statutes.

A special survey in 1961 disclosed that forty-one percent of the public felt that labor leaders who practice featherbedding should be imprisoned and thirty-five percent thought they should not. However, if defense industries are involved, fifty-three percent thought that leaders should be jailed and only twenty-three percent opposed imprisonment.

It is evident that as discussion of the impact of technological change and automation on employment opportunities has continued, public sentiment toward various types of union action to mitigate the effects of displacement has softened. The trend has been in the direction of recognizing the unfavorable plight of workers and the complexities of resolving the difficulties. Unions have been subject to less criticism even for extreme featherbedding activities. It seems that milder forms of makework undertaken by unions are not a cause for much public reproof and censure at the present time.

Government

Government policy in the 1960's, ostensibly devoted to rapid growth of the economy, is hostile to proposals which might curtail output. This is clearly illustrated by Administration opposition to suggestions contemplating a reduction in the hours of work to alleviate unemployment. Ordinarily the government has used its influence against featherbedding practices and legislated against the most flagrant cases, but contrary historical illustrations are available. For example, under the public works program set up by the National Industrial Recovery Act of 1933, Congress stated: "All contracts let for construction projects and all loans and grants pursuant to this title shall contain such provisions as are necessary to insure . . . that the maximum of human labor shall be used in lieu of machinery wherever practicable and consistent with sound economy and public advantage." [25]

In the past thirty years, government policy has supported programs to maintain employment at a level above that warranted by competitive market forces in many instances, although justification for such action has not always been sound. Social and national defense considerations have been urged as warranting special treatment. But state full-crew laws are applicable to the railroads even where safety factors are no longer of significance. Agricultural parity payments have kept many thousands of persons engaged on the farms in unprofitable and unnecessary work. Government subsidy, of course, extends well beyond farming. The maritime and airline industries, for example, receive support which enables them to continue operating at expanded levels. Special advantages are made available to those persons developing certain types of housing projects. Mailing privileges, which shift costs to the general public, assist other enterprises to continue in business. Within its own expanding bureaucracy, the government has long been subject to charges of maintaining excessive employment levels and padded payrolls.[26] It is frequently asserted that civil service laws, which contain rigid tenure provisions, sometimes produce featherbedding situations in government offices.

It is useful to distinguish between those cases where government interference occurs to protect existing employment opportunities and those in which an expansion in the number of employees is intended. It is clear that government monetary expenditures to keep people at work have been made in the past during periods when the economy has been in need of bolstering. Other outlays have been made to provide relief work for persons who have become unemployed. The government now must also seek ways of providing jobs for the new entrants to the labor force who have been finding much difficulty in securing employment during the 1960's.

Some Foreign Experience

Featherbedding is widespread throughout the world and is supported in many countries by statutes which restrict the right of employers to discharge employees. "Featherbedding is a business malaise in many parts of the world, but in Latin America it is a hallowed institution enjoyed by the participants, cheered by the masses and endorsed by the politicians." [27] Such problems are common in many

Latin American industries, including mining, railroading, shipping, oil refining, and automobile manufacturing, and in various South American countries, including Brazil, Argentina, Chile, Peru, and Venezuela. Although in some of these cases workers are resisting displacement caused by technological advance, generally payroll padding is a significant factor. Government support for such activities is not unusual, despite the fact that makework restricts private investment and limits the export market. Political pressures apparently prevail.

In most Western European countries legislation, general contract law, and, in a few cases, collective bargaining agreements have laid down the principle that workers may be dismissed only for valid reasons. A study of the issues involved in this matter concluded that "regardless of the terminology employed—'unjustified,' 'arbitrary,' 'socially unwarranted,' 'abusive,' 'manifestly unreasonable,'—the regulations . . . all seek in their own way to balance the interest of the employer in the efficient operation of the undertaking and the job security interest of the worker." [28] Compensation is the usual remedy for unjustified dismissal in France, Belgium, and Denmark, but a choice between reinstatement and compensation is provided in West Germany, Italy, Belgium, the Netherlands, Sweden, Norway, Spain, and Austria. Workers in Great Britain, however, have no such protection. The principle of justification for dismissals has been evolved during the past fifteen years. Although notice is required before layoff in all Western European countries, severance allowances are much less frequent. Some countries have special statutory enactments for cases involving mass dismissals or layoffs.

EXTENT OF FEATHERBEDDING IN THE ECONOMY

Featherbedding practices, established in formal union rules, are not distributed uniformly through the American economy. They are concentrated occupationally among the more highly skilled workers and industrially in transportation, construction, musical and theatrical entertainment, and newspaper printing. Useless work required in manufacturing stems mainly from the opposition of unions to tightening loose production standards set between 1937 and 1947 as a result of ground-breaking negotiations with newly established unions and from attempts to reestablish business connections rapidly and at any cost in the postwar markets. But much progress has been made in ending these restrictions on output by altering technological processes and gradually readjusting standards.

Although the widespread nature of makework activities is evident and their independence of union existence has been established conclusively, nevertheless featherbedding carried on in systematic fashion has been closely linked to the rules set forth unilaterally or negotiated by labor organizations. Workers are able to engage in featherbedding only if permitted to do so by the employer or strong enough to impose their will upon him. In the former case, action is likely to be temporary and in the latter the behavior pattern of the workers is likely to be developed and crystallized by a union. Occasionally, particularly in construction, pressures on an employer to have a job completed rapidly lead him to accept featherbedding demands by the union in lieu of a strike which would halt operations.

Craft unions, like industrial unions, are anxious to preserve jobs, but they have the further burden of conserving and protecting skills. It is this double objective which makes them more prone to formulate and establish rules which slow down the rate at which work is done and prevent alterations in the methods of production. Craft union attitudes in a sense revert to the protectionism maintained by the medieval guilds. Unions tend to prevent the introduction of new techniques which make skills obsolete because jobs requiring less skill pay lower wages and carry less occupational prestige.

Members of craft unions can exert great pressure for makework regulations because an employer finds it difficult to replace the workers. Since all workers are ordinarily affected equally by any change in technique, they will be unified in their efforts to resist. Industrial unions are less inclined to favor featherbedding practices because advantages derived by one group might be difficult to justify to the other members. Maintaining or increasing employment for one group of workers in the industry, possibly at the cost of not being able to improve the conditions of employment for another group, may be an unwelcome policy to the membership. Too few members are usually affected by any change in technology to make the matter important to the entire membership. Situations which encourage makework practices include those where employment is casual or intermittent, as in longshoring; where the supply of labor is subject to union control, as in printing and entertainment; and where seniority factors are such that some additional employment enables many workers to be upgraded, as in train service on the railroads. Featherbedding is common and work rules which waste resources are frequent in industries where there is rivalry among unions to outdo each other in their demands. Even craft unions, however, must ordinarily concentrate on improvements in wages, hours, and fringe benefits because these issues advance working conditions for all members.

The featherbedding rules of craft unions are intended to maintain or increase the number of jobs and prevent the introduction of greater efficiency. Industrial unions, on the other hand, have been linked to wasteful practices developed slowly over the years, but not deliberately planned or instituted. They have been reluctant, however, to give up advantageous working conditions thus derived.

Featherbedding has been more successful among particular crafts. Typically the craft union is strong. It includes among the membership a substantial proportion of all workers with those skills which differentiate the occupation. Furthermore, since the product market usually is local, competition from other geographical areas does not seriously affect the monopolistic controls and status of the craft unions. Since many of the workers involved are employed in the production of services or in activities where time deadlines are significant, employers are unusually vulnerable to strikes and the exercise of union power.

COSTS OF FEATHERBEDDING

From all indications, the cost of featherbedding is high. Different featherbedding practices carried on tend to increase operating and unit labor costs. The waste which results raises moral issues, but also focuses attention on economic questions. Money losses associated with featherbedding are difficult to determine, though some estimates have had wide currency. The most generally prevalent estimate of the cost of featherbedding to all American industry is an amount of somewhat over $2,000,000,000 per year.[29] According to spokesmen for the industry, about a quarter of this total is borne by the railroads. But claimed railroad losses, originally set at $500,000,000 and more recently increased to $600,000,000 as wage rates have risen, is challenged by labor union officials who contend that if working conditions in the industry were equated to those found in manufacturing by adding overtime payments and various fringe benefits, labor costs might rise by almost three-quarters of a billion dollars.[30] Construction and other transportation sectors are also subject to heavy costs.

Although the number of workers lost as useful members of the labor force as a result of makework practices is greater than appears at first because many work rules are obscure or affect only small groups, the loss of output which results cannot be estimated with any accuracy. It is likely that deliberate makework practices are responsible for the loss of considerably less than a million man-years per year.[31]

The costs of featherbedding are onerous in a competitive economy. Producers involved must meet the challenge of foreign competition where labor may not be imposing work restrictions and a domestic market where substitute products and alternative means of production may become available. United States foreign trade difficulties involve even

those exported products which are free from direct featherbedding restraint. This is because of the added costs American transportation facilities shift forward on those who ship
goods. But restrictions which prevent or reduce technological advance, as distinct from those which add costs
directly, are also of great importance because they tend
to reduce productivity of labor and therefore the competitive strength of American industry.

The costs of makework fall on consumers who pay higher
prices, on workers, management, and owners of enterprise
who receive lower factor payments, and on government in
the form of forgone taxes, higher prices, or bigger subsidies.
Prices in those industries where labor constitutes a larger
fraction of total costs will tend to be more affected by featherbedding, and the market position of the companies will
suffer proportionately. Firms make jobs available when the
relationship of costs to prices is favorable. Makework is not
conducive to expansion in job opportunities. The ordinary
reaction of employers is to seek technological changes and
processes that will not be affected by labor restrictions.
The impact of featherbedding is felt by the economy not
only in higher prices but in limitations on expansion and
growth of industry. Productivity suffers for a variety of
reasons. Output per man-hours paid for is clearly lower as
featherbedding practices cause an increase in man-hours
without any corresponding rise in product. Union rules
which prevent or limit the introduction of new and advanced
technology reduce growth prospects. Cumulative adverse
effects occur because investors ordinarily are reluctant to
put capital into industries where labor restrictions reduce
potential gains. The cost of raising funds thus becomes
higher, and lesser amounts of capital are desired by management. This is particularly important in industries other
than those expanding rapidly. Furthermore, inability of
management to combine resources as it deems most profitable is reinforced by artificial impediments on the movement of labor into those types of work where it is most
urgent from those where its efforts are not needed. Mobility

of labor is hampered by union rules which freeze men in jobs which are obsolete.

The rate of economic growth depends in part on the degree of resource mobility. Effective mobility of labor is hampered when workers are insecure and refuse to abandon jobs even when the work performed is no longer essential. Redundant workers are reluctant to move out of an occupation, industry, or district into another where their services might be urgently required. But this problem, whose solution necessitates financial incentives to employees, retraining programs, and union support, is even more acute in countries where workers receive very little protection than in the United States.[32]

Chapter IV

FEATHERBEDDING: RAILROAD
OPERATING WORKERS

Although the various branches of the transportation industry have experienced considerably different bargaining relationships, almost all of them have been subject to many makework practices. The most publicized and bitter featherbedding dispute has occurred on the railroads, where employers have coordinated their efforts fully and effectively. Elsewhere labor and management have not met in similar head-on struggles. Although fighting among maritime unions has declined in the past few years, bitter rivalries formerly led each of them to resist yielding any ground to employers. Longshoremen were able to secure approval of employers for some of their makework practices as a result of whipsawing tactics by the unions in which favorable terms gained from one company have been used as leverage to obtain equal concessions from other firms. Air carriers, unlike other branches of transportation, have had no common labor policy; the management of each line has acted independently. The trucking industry has opposed featherbedding in collective bargaining negotiations with the teamsters, but it has deliberately done so without publicity or fanfare.

One of the major problems faced by the whole transportation industry in the 1960's is caused by the lack of union responsibility for holding operating costs down. Labor organizations have not been sufficiently concerned to maximize labor productivity and have resisted service adjustments based on user demand and changing technology.[1]

The tendency to impose inflexible and complicated work rules restricting output and operations and reducing the carriers' ability to render efficient service generally permeates transportation labor unions.[2]

The railroad industry, which currently employs about 700,000 workers, is generally considered to provide the most onerous cases of featherbedding. The main issues between management and labor have related to the 200,000 operating employees, that is, those who are employed in work involving moving trains. But some disputes have concerned nonoperating employees—workers who are indirectly involved in train operations. The shopcraft workers, who are employed to maintain and repair rolling stock, have not been involved in featherbedding controversies. But they, unlike operating and nonoperating groups, are able to secure comparable employment in other industries.

ORIGINS OF THE DISPUTE

The rules and practices under which operating railroad workers in the United States are assigned their tasks and paid for their services have been developed during a period extending over 100 years. Lack of immediate supervision called for detailed rules. Since 1875, when the first simple railroad contract was put in written form, the rules have grown in scope and extensiveness and are now incorporated in elaborate and complex collective agreements. The different practices did not all come about from collective bargaining. Many originated in decisions of courts, executive agencies, and arbitration bodies. Others resulted from federal and state legislation. A general examination and evaluation of wages and hours in the railroad industry, which shed much light on operations, was made at the direction of Congress in connection with the Adamson Eight Hour Act of 1916.[3] Prevalent rules and practices were codified by the United States Railroad Administration during and immediately after World War I. Since then, changes have taken place within the framework which was thus established.

The railroad industry was one of the first to be thoroughly organized by unions, and employees achieved relatively good working conditions long before workers in other sectors of the economy were able to obtain them. But the gains of railroad workers have lagged since World War II. During the past twenty years other labor organizations have been able to negotiate great improvements in fringe benefits, while railroad unions have not been very successful in this area.

Vast economic changes have in many ways adversely affected the position of the railroad industry. Reduced profits for many carriers and losses for others have stimulated the search for techniques to lower costs. It is natural, under such conditions, that much attention has been directed toward labor outlays which amount to more than half the total operating revenues of railroads and have been a rising fraction of total costs, despite the almost consistent decline in employment over the past forty years. In 1920 railroads were practically unchallenged as carriers of freight and passengers. Since that time competition has intensified. Automobiles, trucks, buses, airplanes, ships, and pipelines have garnered ever larger shares of the passenger and freight business. Railroad traffic has changed: more bulk cargo and less general merchandise is moved; long hauls have increased in relation to short hauls; and freight represents a greater proportion of the service.

The railroad industry originated and developed as a result of technological advance, but displacement of workers was relatively unimportant for a long time because expansion of the industry enlarged the labor market until 1920. Since then, the impact of technology has been different. Changes of many kinds have altered the character of tasks and duties of employees and have reduced the number of employees required. The increased use of diesel engines, the increased size and power of locomotive engines, the greater capacity of cars, and the improvements in rails and roadbeds have led to longer, heavier, and faster trains. Accidents and delays have been reduced by the use of electronic and mechanical devices which locate defects and hazards. Telephone and radio communication have replaced the telegraph and have brought major modifications in road operations. Other important technological advances include centralized traffic control systems and yard automation.

Technological developments, competitive pressures, and the severe and prolonged economic depression which began in 1929 all contributed to the continual decline in railroad employment (except for the war years) that started in 1920. All groups suffered. Between 1948 and 1960 the number of jobs for operating workers—engineers, firemen, conductors, brakemen, and switchtenders—fell from about 300,000 to 200,000, though the relative decline for nonoperating workers was much greater.

New prevalent bargaining patterns developed by American unions and substantial economic and technological changes in the railroad industry have led to almost universal recognition that basic working rules formulated forty years ago are no longer appropriate or applicable. A complete overhaul is in order.

Featherbedding on the railroads stems from work rules which have become obsolete because they have hardly been altered since they were developed more than forty years ago. Full-crew laws in almost half the states specify the number of brakemen and other crew positions required on freight and passenger trains. Interpretations of contract provisions and work rules by arbitrators and referees have modified the original intent of agreements and forbidden some labor-saving changes.

For many years work-rule problems have been a recurrent and almost routine feature of collective bargaining negotiations in the industry. The carriers ordinarily demand modification or elimination of some of the rules. In return for withdrawing these requests, the unions reduce their wage demands. This exchange has been called "selling the rules."

The railroads are bound to use the minimum number of men prescribed in full-crew laws, but they exercise considerable discretion in regulating engine, train, and switching crews on many matters closely linked to safety. Carriers determine the duties and responsibilities of each crew member, the position on the train at which each member is stationed and performs his work, and the training and experience necessary to qualify for any operating job classification. Flexibility in these respects is in sharp contrast to rigidities in the size of the crew.

Although negotiated rules and state laws have provided most of the employment which is in dispute, decisions of the National Railroad Adjustment Board, which handles grievances in the railroad industry, are responsible for some of it. Many rigidities in job assignments of road and yard crews have resulted from contract interpretations made by the NRAB. On the basis of seniority rules, for example, the Board adopted the policy of assigning property rights to work. Each piece of work belongs to a class of labor, a member of which must be called upon to perform it, regardless of whether it can be performed more expeditiously and efficiently by others. This has provided work for yard crews even when yards have been abolished.[4] Similarly, much duplication of employment on maintenance-of-way equipment results from rulings of the NRAB.

Only during World War II, when severe manpower shortages developed in the railroad industry, did the unions relax some of their rules. At that time, the United States Office of Defense Transportation was able to secure an informal understanding from the unions that some of the makework rules would not be strictly enforced. The program included relaxation of mileage limitations on road crews and hourly limitations on yard service employees. Yard operating rules were eased to allow crews bringing cars to the tracks or yards of another road to haul back cars to their own road so that the engine would pull a load in both directions.[5] While some employees, particularly those in local freight service, worked more than sixty hours a week, passenger train engine service employees averaged fewer than forty hours a week.

Generally, however, management and the unions have been in sharp disagreement over work rules. The railroad carriers have charged that the antiquated wage structure and manning requirements of the industry incorporate many featherbedding elements.

Between 1917 and 1920, when the federal government operated the railroads, a four-man Railroad Wage Commission (the Lane Commission) appointed by the Director General of Railroads made recommendations regarding wages of railroad labor. These were adopted in essence and put into effect in 1918 in General Order 27 of the United States Railroad Administration. The following year, the wage provisions were supplemented as a result of recommendations made by an advisory board on railroad wages and working conditions. The board was composed of carrier and union representatives. The combined efforts of these two groups have constituted the last comprehensive examination and standardization of the railroad wage structure in the industry. The most recent systematic study and survey of the wage rate structure in the train and engine service of the railroads was made by the United States Federal Coordinator of Transportation in March, 1936.

In 1955 an emergency board, appointed under the Railway Labor Act to investigate a dispute concerning wage rates of operating train service employees, found the railroad wage structure "obsolete and ill-designed for a modern railroad system" and declared that there was an imperative need for a thoroughgoing review and modernization of the wage structure.[6] Such a study, it said, is essential to correct wage inequities, to improve industrial relations, and to permit efficient operation of the railroads.

Some of the most complicated railroad rules deal with the dual system of pay. Daily or monthly wages, the original method of remuneration, proved unsatisfactory because they failed to provide incentives for operating employees to work at top speed. The trip-rate and mileage-pay systems which followed were more suitable to the needs of the carriers. The dual basis of payment, begun in the 1880's, combined mileage and hours in computing earnings. It was standardized during the years the federal government operated the railroads. Since then, a basic day's wage has been paid to engineers and firemen in passenger engine service for work involving not more than either 100 miles or five hours; to passenger train service brakemen and conductors for work involving not more than either 150 miles or seven and a half hours; and to all freight service employees for work involving not more than either 100 miles or eight hours. Overtime per hour for freight service employees is one and a half times straight-time rates, and for passenger service employees it is an eighth of the daily rates. Other payments known as guarantees, constructive allowances, and arbitraries are added.

The standards of 100 and 150 miles were set at a time when the average speed of trains was less than half what it is now. But technological advance which led to increased train speeds made the mileage basis of pay obsolete. As a result, wage costs rose and many railroad operating employees are able to earn a basic day's pay in two hours or less. The system of payment has become a source of great inequity among railroad workers and has led to many strange results. One of the most publicized examples, although not typical, concerns the 452-mile round-trip between New York City and Washington, D. C., which fast passenger trains run in less than eight hours. Engineers and firemen receive four and a half basic days' wages for the actual train running time. Other comparable situations exist elsewhere.

The most notorious instance of featherbedding by the operating railroad employees has been the requirement that an excessive number of workers should be employed. Though this objective was gained to a large extent from statutory action,[7] collective bargaining has also played a role. At first a desire to make promotion easier for the workers led the railroad unions to demand larger crews. Subsequently, declining employment and technological displacement provided the incentives.

When diesels were first introduced in road service about 1934,[8] some carriers felt that firemen were not equipped by training or experience to supervise the power plant in the locomotive. The carriers assigned skilled shopcraft employees to this function. Many of the early diesel passenger trains operated without a fireman or, as he is now called, "fireman (helper)."[9] This situation was comparable to rail motor cars which had long been operated by an engineer alone.

Diesel locomotives are powered by internal combustion engines and differ greatly from steam locomotives. The function of the fireman—to supply fuel to the firebox on steam locomotives—is eliminated and a new kind of work —attention to the engine room—differing from operating tasks performed on all other types of power engines comes into existence. The only fire used on diesel-powered trains is one that provides heat and hot water for passengers, but this is now regulated from the cab. The obvious threat posed by this superior and more efficient form of power to the jobs of locomotive firemen in yard, freight, and passenger service was of grave concern to the union.

The locomotive firemen's union was able to conclude a number of agreements with individual carriers in 1935 and 1936. These agreements provided for the employment of a "fireman (helper)" on diesel locomotives. The duties of the position were to assist the engineer in the cab and the maintainer in the engine room. Sharp lines governing jurisdiction among the crafts were not drawn. The union completed the program of safeguarding the jobs of its members by negotiating a national diesel agreement, dated February 28, 1937, under which a fireman had to be employed on locomotives of all types of power in road and yard service. Only diesels with a weight on drivers, which is the weight borne by the power-driven axles of the locomotives, of 90,000 pounds or less, and electric trains used for commuters were exempt. Duties to be performed by firemen on diesels were not specified in the contract.

The union estimated that the agreement required the railroads to hire about 230 additional helpers immediately. At that time, there were 43,624 steam locomotives compared to 218 diesels in use on Class I railroads. Although few persons anticipated that diesel locomotives would supplant steam very rapidly, by 1959, when management opened the big battle against featherbedding, there were 28,163 diesels and only 754 steam locomotives.

The engineers, in 1937, and the firemen, in 1941, undertook campaigns to increase the number of men in the cab. Each union claimed that the presence of a third man was necessary for the efficient operation of diesels; each insisted that its roster was the appropriate one for the carriers to use when making a selection. The moves were prompted by fear that the diesel was a serious threat to employment security. Diesels had become more powerful, operating in multiple units, and by that time had been introduced into freight service. Negotiation of the demands made by the unions was unsuccessful, and mediation also failed. The services of an emergency board were required to investigate the demands of each of the two unions. The report of the board, made in 1943, was against an increase in the standard two-man engine crew.[10] It did state that multiple-unit diesel, high-speed, main-line through passenger trains require as a safety measure that a fireman should be in the cab whenever the train is in motion. In this restricted situation another fireman might be necessary to perform engine room service. But if there was no more than one fireman on the train, he could leave the cab only when the train stopped.

Following the report and further negotiations, contracts significantly cognizant of these recommendations were signed by the firemen in 1943 and by the engineers in 1944 with both the eastern conference of carriers and western conference of carriers and by the firemen in 1944 and by the engineers in 1945 with the southeastern conference. In 1945 the engineers again raised the question of another man on diesel locomotives. Two years later the firemen demanded a change in the rules which would add a second fireman on diesel locomotives in road service and would require a fireman in yard service on diesel locomotives weighing 90,000 pounds or less on drivers. Following a period of bargaining in which the National Mediation Board intervened, an emergency board was appointed for each of the two controversies. Both reported in 1949, and both rejected the demands of engineers and firemen for additional men on diesels.[11]

The unions were unhappy with the recommendations. After further and prolonged negotiation, they signed contracts, although a short strike by the firemen on some of the carriers did occur for several days prior to completion on May 16, 1950 of an agreement to arbitrate some questions. The manning issue remained relatively dormant until 1956, when the carriers proposed elimination of firemen on diesels in road freight and yard service. The demand was withdrawn late in the year as part of the contract settlement and a three-year moratorium on rules changes was instituted. In 1959, at the end of the period, the contract was coming up for renegotiation, and the railroads requested changes in working rules which would give management the right to decide when firemen should be employed on diesels in freight and yard service.

The position of American railroad management in 1959 in tackling the featherbedding issue had been considerably strengthened as a result of Canadian experience in the years immediately preceding. The success of Canadian railroads in eliminating firemen from diesel trains spurred American carriers to press the same issue more firmly. In 1948 an agreement had been signed between the Canadian Pacific Railway Company (CPR) and the Brotherhood of Locomotive Firemen and Enginemen requiring the employment of a fireman on all diesel locomotives with a weight on drivers of more than 90,000 pounds. On February 6, 1956, shortly after negotiations for a new contract began, the CPR informed the union that it wished to eliminate all rules and practices requiring firemen on diesel locomotives

in freight and yard service. The company considered such
employment featherbedding and makework. Freight trains
carry three men in the cab—an engineer, fireman, and head-
end trainman—but passenger trains use only an engineer
and fireman.

The impasse which followed led to the appointment of a
conciliation board by the Minister of Labour. On December
17, 1956, the board recommended that the company should
be permitted to drop firemen providing it protected the
jobs of those with three years or more of seniority and paid
monetary compensation to the others. Though the company
accepted the report, the union did not. A poll of the members of the union brought unanimous agreement authorizing
a strike. On January 2, 1957, the strike began. About 2,800
firemen were involved, but 60,000 employees of the line
were idled as CPR rail operations were shut down.

The strike ended on January 11 when the parties agreed
to negotiate the issue on the basis of an advisory report
which would be made by a royal commission established
for this purpose. The three-man commission was appointed
later in the month under the chairmanship of Justice Roy L.
Kellock. Hearings were held through most of 1957. Members of the commission made personal observations of operations, rode in the cabs of road and yard service diesel
locomotives, and visited several European countries to make
comparisons. The report was completed on December 18,
1957,[12] but was not issued by the government until February
4, 1958.

The commission found that the weight on the driver was
irrelevant in considering the need for a fireman. It concluded that firemen are not required to transmit signals to
the engineer, to perform lookout duty, to provide mechanical
assistance, or to relieve engineers on diesel locomotives in
freight and yard service. Furthermore, the commission declared that diesel locomotives in the United Kingdom,
France, Switzerland, and the Netherlands, are with few
exceptions operated in passenger, freight, and yard service
without firemen and neither safety nor efficiency have been

shown to be adversely affected. On the whole, the commission agreed with the conciliation board and supported the company's position. Firemen with seniority prior to April 1, 1953 were to retain their jobs, but they would not be replaced if their employment ceased or they were promoted; others would be offered employment as trainmen or yardmen, except that those with seniority commencing subsequent to March 31, 1956 would be entitled only to preference over new applicants for employment.

In 1956, the CPR employed an average of about 2,927 firemen—449 in passenger service, 1,690 in freight service, and 788 in yard service. Under the recommendations, jobs of about 1,900 (increased to 2,378 in the final settlement) of the 2,478 in freight and yard service would not have been affected at all, and only about 100 were not assured of getting other positions. The carrier, whose net railway operating income was $41,336,000 in 1956, estimated that these changes would effect an annual saving of $5,746,000.[13]

After renewed negotiations broke down, the company announced that the recommendations would be implemented on May 11, 1958. The firemen's union called a strike for that day. But the stoppage failed, in part because injunctions against cessation of work were issued in several provinces, in part because support from the other unions was not forthcoming, and in part because public opinion considered the company to be right and the union wrong. Picket lines set up by the firemen were not honored by other workers. Within three days, the parties came to terms and signed a contract incorporating the recommendations of the Kellock commission. The union agreed that firemen need no longer be hired on diesel trains in freight and yard service. But it gained one important new concession in the final settlement. Jobs of all firemen with seniority prior to April 1, 1956 were protected.[14]

The process of attrition has worked slowly at CPR. On April 1, 1958, there were 2,637 firemen with seniority antedating April 1, 1956. Three years later the number had been reduced by about twenty-three percent.

The issue concerning the employment of firemen then shifted to the Canadian National Railway Company. Although the union threatened to strike when a governmental conciliation board investigating the dispute made recommendations similar to those of the Kellock commission, it did not do so because the other operating unions were opposed to such action. In April, 1959 the firemen were forced to accept terms similar to those reached with CPR and the matter of employment of firemen on diesels in freight and yard service was settled in Canada.[15]

On February 10, 1959, Daniel P. Loomis, president of the Association of American Railroads, asked the five operating railroad unions to support the establishment of a presidential commission to examine and report on the working rules of the industry. On May 18, the Interstate Commerce Commission in a report dealing with railroad passenger traffic deficits declared that examination and revision of working rules in the railroad industry was necessary to eliminate unjustifiably uneconomic use of labor.[16] The proposal made by Loomis was turned down by the unions on June 4 in letters written to him and to the Secretary of Labor. On August 17, Loomis wrote to President Dwight D. Eisenhower that the three-year moratorium on work-rules changes was expiring on October 31 and that the appointment of a commission to examine the problems and make recommendations was advisable. On August 24, the unions declared their opposition to such a commission. As a result, on September 9, the President decided not to appoint one.

The vigorous campaign launched in 1959 against the makework practices of operating employees and the basis of wage payments stemmed mainly from the increased competition besetting the railroads. Railroad spokesmen contended that the outmoded working rules drained in excess of $500,000,000 from the industry each year[17] (the figure was raised to $600,000,000 in 1962), restricted technological improvements, and lessened job opportunities. Management asked for a revision of the wage structure, which was tied to the number of hours or miles a man worked each week, and manning requirements, which involved the number of persons employed, the types of jobs performed, and the skills necessary to operate a train. More specifically, the carriers wished to increase the mileage coverage necessary for a basic day's pay from 100 to 160, abolish the job of fireman in freight and yard service, allow labor to be interchanged between road and yard crews, permit management to determine the size of crews, eliminate multiple crew changes required at interdivisional points, and end the practice requiring idle standby employees when self-propelled equipment is used.

Personnel reductions were demanded in both engine and train service. The locomotive cab crew in freight road service would be reduced from three men—engineer, brakeman, and fireman—to two and in yard service from two men —engineer and fireman—to one. The crews of locomotives in passenger road service, consisting of an engineer and fireman, would not be affected. The train complement in road and yard service ordinarily consists of one conductor and two brakemen outside the cab. The railroads want a national rule giving them the unrestricted right to determine appropriate crew size. Unions want a rule to establish the principle that three men represent the *minimum* crew for all trains.

An industry study released at the end of 1959 showed: that staffing "unnecessary" positions required $280,000,000, including $230,000,000 for surplus firemen in yard and freight service and $50,000,000 for other unnecessary jobs in connection with train service (such as those required by state full-crew laws) and work machinery; that the obsolete pay system for train crews set in accordance with the number of miles covered increased the payroll by $150,-000,000; and that duplication of work and wage payments related to union jurisdictional work rules and barriers which prevent yard crews from working on the road and vice versa and which bar railroads from extending crew runs beyond division points added $120,000,000.[18]

Management felt that revised work rules would permit the elimination of more than 60,000 of the 200,000 train and engine service jobs. The largest group facing dismissal were the thousands of firemen employed on freight and yard diesel locomotives. Many more thousands of jobs could be terminated if a day's work were increased from 100 miles to 160 miles and if the size of train crews were reduced.

Two days after the expiration of the moratorium, on November 2, 1959, the carriers served notice on the unions, as required by Section 6 of the Railway Labor Act, that they intended to change the contract terms affecting rates of pay, rules, and working conditions. The proposed changes contemplated eliminating "firemen (helpers)" on other than steam locomotives when used in yard and freight service; altering the basis of pay and the assignment of operating employees used in through-freight and straightaway passenger service; reconstituting the composition of crews on the road and in yards; and removing operating employees from self-propelled machines used in inspection and maintenance work. An entirely different group of changes in the rules were included in the counterproposals made by the unions on September 7, 1960.

THE PRESIDENTIAL RAILROAD COMMISSION

After a long series of rather fruitless conferences on the issues took place, the parties agreed on October 17, 1960, under the guidance of Secretary of Labor James P. Mitchell, to the creation of a Presidential Railroad Commission which would investigate and report on the controversy and attempt to bring about an amicable settlement. Executive Order 10891 of November 1, 1960 created a Commission of fifteen members, five appointed from nominations by the unions, five from nominations by the carriers, and five public members chosen without nominations by the parties. Designations were made by the President on December 22, and hearings began on February 16, 1961. Secretary of Labor Mitchell, who was named chairman, resigned soon after his appointment and was replaced by Simon H. Rifkind. The Commission heard oral testimony which fills more than 15,300 printed pages and received more than 20,000 additional pages of exhibits. Field trips were made and actual train rides were taken by the neutral members to gain firsthand information about working conditions on the railroads. The Commission staff and consultants conducted many independent studies of railroad labor problems. At the end of 1961, after the hearings had been concluded, the public members tried to mediate the dispute, but their efforts were unsuccessful. The report and recommendations of the Commission were submitted to the President on February 28, 1962. Specific changes in the rules were proposed and methods of protecting employees adversely affected were included.[19]

The inquiry made by the Presidential Railroad Commission concerning the pay structure and working rules of operating employees on railroads was the most comprehensive ever undertaken. The issues involved the structure of the compensation system, manning of trains and engines, assignment of employees, and provisions for employee security. The Commission prescribed changes for the industry based upon the general conclusions it reached. It suggested revision of the rules governing manning of trains and engines and the assignment of employees so that unnecessary jobs would be eliminated, subject to safeguards for adversely affected workers; overhaul of the entire complicated system of compensation; and modification in the procedures for disposing grievances and administering rules.

The Commission found that the railroad unions were trying to protect jobs and incomes threatened by technological change, by the adverse effects of the business cycle, and by competitive enterprise. The unions did not permit changes without negotiation of each rule, and generally threatened to resort to the strike in these cases. Management, however, wished unrestricted control to introduce changes without the need to negotiate. It considered technological displacement a hazard of industrial life against

which workers were to be protected generally only by unemployment compensation. The view of the Commission
was that the cost of plans to protect employees displaced by
machinery should be charged against the savings resulting
from technological advance, and that benefits should include
specified monthly allowances or lump sums, retraining sub-
ventions, and preferential hiring status. However, carriers
unable to work out agreements with the unions regarding
changes should have the option of submitting the question
to a special tribunal of neutrals set up on a national basis
for final and binding determination.

The Commission found a declining need for operating
employees in the railroad industry and recommended that
the adjustment would be more orderly if agreements would
be negotiated to provide for mandatory retirement at age
sixty-five. The situation was particularly bad among the
senior employees—engineers and conductors. In 1959, the
median age was fifty-nine for engineers and fifty-three for
conductors. Five percent of the engineers and six percent
of the conductors were over seventy years of age and an
additional seventeen percent of engineers and nine percent
of conductors were between sixty-five and seventy years old.
In part, the condition arose because employees with long
seniority choose the "red-apple" runs—those in which wages
are high for very short workdays. Workers consider themselves entitled to these lucrative jobs after they have put in
many years of service and are less likely to retire once such
positions have been gained.

Elimination of the fireman's job would become practical
if more engineers retired, since engineers are normally re-
cruited from among the firemen. Furthermore, merger of
the engineers' union and firemen's union would simplify the
problem. But though the firemen have on several occasions
in the past sought such consolidation, unification has been
rejected by the smaller and wealthier locomotive engineers'
union.

The Commission recommended the elimination of firemen on road freight and yard diesels. It rejected the argu-

ment that they are necessary for safe and efficient operation in relieving the engineer or performing lookout and mechanical functions. (In road service, a head-end brakeman also rides with the engineer in the cab and in yard service, ground crews work alongside the locomotive.) The Commission felt that the composition or consist of road and yard service crews should be determined by collective bargaining subject to final and binding arbitration if no agreement could be reached in a specified period. The main categories of workers involved in this issue are road brakemen and yard helpers. The Commission further recommended that carriers should be free from any rules requiring assignment of operating employees to motor cars and self-propelled vehicles used for construction, maintenance, or inspection which utilize the services of other crews of railroad workers.

Far-reaching comments were made with respect to the role of management in the assignment of employees. The Commission favored elimination of rules which prevent carriers from relocating crew terminals and altering interdivisional runs. While indicating that mobility has been characteristic of many types of employment, it was concerned with the uprooting and relocation of families, reduced market value of workers' homes, and costs of moving to new communities attendant upon changing terminal points. Yet progress was found to be necessary. The Commission proposed easing the rigid regulations which separate the work of road service from yard service and suggested that the interchange of work between these groups should be authorized. Such modifications, it said, would bring greater efficiency and substantial reduction in costs.

The Presidential Railroad Commission devoted much attention to the wage structure of the industry and concluded that it was chaotic. It found a need to alter the unconscionable disparity in hours on duty, inconsistencies in overtime schedules based on speed, anomalies in the dual basis of pay, and inequities in compensation differentials among and within the classes of service. Structural deficiencies and inadequacies, it said, had been made possible by the acquiescence of those employees benefiting from seniority advantages involving the choice of assignments. A complete overhaul of the most complicated wage system of any major industry in the United States was found necessary. Appropriate changes to rectify unfair conditions and simplify the basis of compensation were recommended.

The Commission estimated that its proposals to revise the pay structure would bring higher earnings to about seventy-five percent of operating employees, including almost all in yard and local freight service, those working long hours in all categories, and road employees on short runs. The twenty-five percent of employees whose work trips cover more than 100 hundred miles in less than eight hours would receive lower earnings, but the effects would be minimized from a somewhat longer work week. The proposed structural revision would bring an increase of about two percent in freight and yard service earnings.

The Commission suggested that gradual and orderly adjustments in the working conditions of employees of the railroad industry were desirable and that there was need for more vigorous and highly trained management, greater coherence in the national transportation policy of the government, and improved procedures for administering grievances and claims. But it stressed that labor relations and the best interests of the employees in the industry could be furthered only if, in the immediate future, the five separate unions of operating employees would merge into two organizations comprising train service employees, on the one hand, and engine service employees on the other. It seemed clear that many of the featherbedding issues and problems stemmed from the overlapping and confined jurisdictions of the trade unions involved.

Fear that the long-term downward trend in railroad employment would continue led the unions to fight vigorously against the antifeatherbedding campaign of the railroads. At the outset, in 1959, the brotherhoods severely criticized what they labeled management featherbedding. They stressed that the number of management employees had not declined during a period when overall employment in the railroad industry had dropped by almost fifty percent. But the carriers simply contended that the greater complexity of plant, equipment, and operating methods required relatively more supervisory talent. They added that despite a decline of one-half in the membership of the five operating unions since the early 1920's, the number of vice presidents in these organizations increased from thirty-nine to sixty-three between 1923 and 1959.[20]

Union representatives claim that elimination of those rules objectionable to the carriers is unlikely to reduce operating costs by the $500,000,000 or $600,000,000 the carriers estimated. On the contrary, they contend that conversion of the wage system to an hourly basis would add about $647,000,000 in costs[21] for overtime, night-shift and holiday premiums, additional fringes common in other industries, and severance pay for displaced workers.[22] It should be noted that an appraisal of the divergent estimates is difficult to make because of the overlapping calculations and the extra payments that would be incurred in a reorganization of the wage structure. Actually, of the 200,000 operating workers, about 100,000 are now engaged in yard service and are paid on an hourly basis.

The report of the Presidential Railroad Commission does not reflect the bitterness and strife between labor and management which the work of this body intensified. Fortunately, some of the sentiment has been preserved because the Commission member representing the locomotive engineers refused to sign the report to the President which his colleagues submitted and instead, prepared his own 114-page document which contains much crimination and some material not found elsewhere.[23] The public members of the Commission were sharply criticized for preconceived and intransigent notions, poor attendance at hearings and plenary sessions, and being unduly influenced by public opinion. The union member wrote: "The report is the patchwork assembly of the five public members, unidentified staff, and undisclosed self-serving sources of information and judgment." From the outset there were disagreements between the labor members and the others regarding the name and procedures to be used by the Commission. Labor wanted emphasis on study and mediation; the other members favored an adversary approach. In each case, the views favored by labor representatives were rejected. The report and recommendations of the Commission were found unacceptable by the rail unions as a basis for collective bargaining.

National conferences between the parties were resumed on April 2, 1962, and continued through May 17 without agreement. Although the report and recommendations of the Commission were accepted by the carriers, they were rejected by the unions. Between May 25 and June 22, about thirty-two more meetings were held under the auspices of the National Mediation Board, but again without success. The railroad companies agreed to the NMB proposal that the dispute be arbitrated, but the unions refused to agree. On July 16, the NMB terminated its services under provisions of the Railway Labor Act. The following day, the railroads notified the unions that changes in rates of pay, rules, and working conditions would be put into effect on August 16. Subsequently, the railroad companies decided that the changes would be those they had originally set forth on November 2, 1959. The five operating unions brought suit in the United States District Court for the Northern District of Illinois, contending that the proposed unilateral changes in the rules violated the principle in the Railway Labor Act which requires collective bargaining. The District Court, which dismissed the complaint, was upheld by the Circuit Court of Appeals on November 28.[24] However, the companies were forestalled from effectuating any revision of the rules when the District Court granted an injunction, upheld by the Circuit Court, against any change during the period in which the union appeal was pending in the courts.[25]

THE EMERGENCY BOARD

The United States Supreme Court upheld the decisions of the lower courts on March 4, 1963.[26] In a unanimous (per curiam) opinion the court found that the parties had exhausted all the statutory procedures and were therefore free to pursue self-help measures, subject only to the provisions of Section 10 of the Railway Labor Act, under which the President could create an emergency board. Unilateral imposition of changes in working rules by the carriers did not violate the law. The District Court thereupon dissolved the injunction that prevented the railroads from posting the changes.

The carriers then decided to impose the new work rules on April 8, and in order to forestall a threatened strike by the five operating unions, President John F. Kennedy appointed an emergency board under provisions of the Railway Labor Act on April 3. Samuel I. Rosenman was named chairman.

The three members of the board considered their main function to be to bring about a mediated settlement, and toward that end they looked for new approaches to resolve the dispute. They noted that a strike or lockout would idle ninety-four percent of the industry's employees, bring to a halt the movement of passengers and freight over ninety-two percent of the rail mileage, and cause untold damage to the economy of the nation. But the board found productivity of labor rising rapidly and earning capacity of the railroads improving. When it issued its report on May 13, 1963,[27] it felt that the climate for negotiation between the parties had become somewhat better. The chairman indicated that the alternatives to a private settlement of the issues would be Congressional authorization for either compulsory arbitration or governmental seizure of the railroads.

The board liberalized and softened many of the recommendations of the Presidential Railroad Commission. The report of the emergency board was much more palatable to the unions as a basis for bargaining than the findings of the Presidential Railroad Commission had been. The carriers, on the other hand, were willing to accept the recommendations without qualifications. Further negotiation, however, achieved few results.

On June 13 the parties were free to take action under the Railway Labor Act—carriers to put rules changes into effect and unions to strike. The intervention of the Secretary of Labor and federal mediators, however, postponed the date on which the railroad carriers determined to post new work rules to June 18. Shortly before this deadline, President Kennedy prevailed upon the parties to defer action until July 11, indicating that they must settle the dispute themselves or face governmental legislation.

THE LAW

Once again, early in July, a strike on 195 railroads appeared imminent—all major roads were involved except the Southern Railway Company which bargains separately on the rule change issues. On July 8, the rail unions rejected and the carriers accepted a proposal made by Secretary of Labor Wirtz three days earlier to implement by negotiation and arbitration over the succeeding two years the principles laid down by the emergency board concerning firemen and crew composition. On July 9, one day after the unions turned down the Wirtz plan, President Kennedy took a hand. He suggested that the issues be submitted for final settlement to Associate Justice of the Supreme Court Arthur J. Goldberg. The following day, the carriers accepted the plan, but the five rail unions, strongly objecting to arbitration, turned it down.

The impending rules changes and the resulting work stoppage were only eight hours away when the President asked both sides to postpone action through July 29, assuring them that he would ask no further extensions from them. In the interim he proposed to set up a subcommittee of six men selected from the President's Advisory Committee on Labor-Management Policy. This group would make a comprehensive review of the rules dispute. Based on the report, President Kennedy said, he would make recommendations to the legislature on July 22. Congress would then have until July 29 to act. Both sides accepted the postponement. Kennedy selected Secretary of Labor Wirtz as chairman of the group of six. The other members were the Secretary of Commerce, two representatives from management, and two from labor.

The subcommittee outlined the positions of the parties on the eight issues in the dispute. The main difficulties involved the employment of firemen and the composition of crews. The unions, it found, maintain that combination of road and yard work should be handled locally, while the carriers want minimum criteria developed. The manning of motor cars and self-propelled vehicles, interdivisional runs, compensation (wage structure and fringe benefits), employment security, and formal apprenticeship training programs for engine service employees apparently would be resolved, the subcommittee felt, if the other three issues were settled.[28]

On July 22, three days after receiving the unanimous report from the subcommittee, the President submitted recommendations to Congress for resolution of the controversy. In his message to Congress, Kennedy contended that the cost of an extended nationwide rail strike to the public would be intolerable and in very short order would create widespread economic chaos and distress. He said: "These issues, unlike those of typical wage disputes, are ones with very little collective-bargaining play left in them. The work-rules aspects of the present dispute are regarded as do-or-die matters by both parties—and the history of industrial relations shows that when employers and employees consider the issue to be this vital, they can both stand a strike much longer than the country can stand it."[29] Rejecting governmental seizure of the railroads as creating unduly complex legal and financial problems and rejecting compulsory arbitration as inconsistent with free collective bargaining, the President proposed that Congress should turn over the dispute to the Interstate Commerce Commission for solution. The ICC, he said, is already assigned the function of determining specific terms and conditions of employment to protect the job security of workers when railroad mergers are approved under the Interstate Commerce Act. The ICC would be given power for two years to approve, reject, or modify work rules upon which the parties cannot agree. Each submission to it would be acted upon within four months or as soon thereafter as is practicable, the decision being guided by the work and conclusions of the Presidential Railroad Commission and the emergency board. The parties would be free to change any rule imposed by the ICC through agreement, but injunctions would prevent strikes or lockouts intended to bypass these legal provisions. The statute would expire in two years unless extended by Congress.

Congressional leadership prevailed upon the railroads to postpone once again, for another month, until August 29, modification of the work rules, while the House and the Senate each conducted hearings and considered legislation. In mid-August, it appeared briefly that the unions had reversed themselves and accepted a proposal by Secretary Wirtz to arbitrate the key matters of firemen's jobs and composition of train crews. But when agreement could not be reached on the specific definitions of the questions to be submitted and the procedures to be followed in disposing of the other issues, voluntary arbitration had to be discarded.

Congress, however, refused to accept President Kennedy's idea that the ICC should determine the issues. It also rejected suggestions by the unions that a Congressional watchdog committee should be set up to supervise continued negotiations between the parties. Senator Wayne L. Morse, who had served as chairman of a railroad emergency board in 1941, was quite critical of the brotherhoods. In 1951, at Senate hearings, he had said that railroad work rules which involve makework and inefficiency should be annulled and that arbitration is the proper means of settling such issues.[30] Morse, one of the two Senators voting against the railroad labor law subsequently passed by Congress, said that the brotherhoods were stalling because they wanted to maintain the *status quo*. The union leaders, he added, although desiring compulsory arbitration, were fearful of taking responsibility for such action and were anxious to make Congress the scapegoat. Morse scathingly denounced the lobbying pressures exerted by the railroad unions.[31]

The unions, of course, were taking advantage of their strategic position. George Meany, president of the AFL-CIO, pointed out to the Senate committee conducting hearings that the unions and their members were disposed to strike in the railroad controversy because issues and circumstances were unusual. Ordinarily employees weigh whether they will win a strike and make gains or lose and sustain losses. In this instance, if they lose a strike they are no worse off, because their jobs would be eliminated in any event.

On August 28, 1963, Congress passed, and the President signed, a measure which provides for arbitration of the two main issues—the need for the 32,000 firemen on diesel locomotives in freight and yard service and the size of train crews involving 19,000 jobs, mostly brakemen and yard helpers—and bars a strike for 180 days. In unprecedented action, the law calls for compulsory arbitration of a labor-management dispute in peacetime. The statute sets forth a specific procedure to be followed. Within five days after enactment, each party is to name two arbitrators, and these four in turn will then select three neutral members. Should agreement on the choice of any of the members not be possible, the President is directed to make the designations within ten days after passage of the law. The seven-man tripartite board must begin its deliberations no later than thirty days after the enactment of the law. Sixty days thereafter, subsequent to hearings, the board is to make an award which becomes effective sixty days later. The award is binding for two years from the date it becomes effective, unless the parties to the dispute agree otherwise. The law expires 180 days after enactment, but during this period unilateral changes in working conditions by the carriers or strikes by the workers are prohibited and subject to court injunction. The statute provides that the other issues in the controversy should be resolved by collective bargaining.

The seven-man arbitration board, whose three neutral members were named by President Kennedy, was headed by Ralph T. Seward. On November 26, 1963, it made its award.[32] The board ruled that about ninety percent of diesel firemen's jobs in freight and yard service are unnecessary and might be eliminated by the carriers as attrition permits. Firemen with ten years of seniority or more (about sixty-five percent of firemen) retain their rights to continued employment in the same position. Those with less than ten but more than two years of seniority also retain such rights unless offered comparable jobs. Other firemen may be separated, but in some of these cases severance allowances must be paid.

The issue relating to the size of train crews was remanded by the board to local negotiation. Procedures for review and change are applicable where employment conditions require any number other than two trainmen. If no agreement can be reached at the local level, final and binding arbitration procedures based on guidelines laid down by the board are to follow. Jobs of conductors are not affected, but other categories of trainmen, including assistant conductors, ticket collectors, baggagemen, brakemen, and flagmen, come under terms of the award.

The two union representatives on the board dissented vigorously. Four of the five operating railroad unions sued to bar implementation of the board's ruling. The conductors' union did not join in the suit because only a few of its members were affected by the award. On January 8, 1964, a federal district court upheld the award. But the railroads agreed to postpone the effective date of the arbitration award until the courts had decided the appeal by the unions. On February 20, the United States Circuit Court of Appeals for the District of Columbia upheld the judgment of the district court that Congress had the power to order arbitration in the rail dispute, that the arbitration board had acted within the orbit of the authority delegated to it, and that the award was valid.[33]

The controversy concerning the appropriate number of operating employees to man the railroads, which began in 1959, is now more than five years old. While the carriers are now in a much stronger position, they still face legal battles and collective bargaining struggles before they can completely eliminate "unnecessary" employees.

SPECIAL PROBLEMS

The dispute between the firemen and Southern Railway Company took a peculiar turn. This carrier was not a party to the initial diesel manpower agreement reached in 1937 between the union and a number of Class I railroads, but it approved the southeastern agreement of 1944 which contained a section requiring employment on all locomotives of a fireman or helper taken from the seniority ranks of firemen. Some difficulty ensued subsequent to June 30, 1947, at which time the union sought to incorporate new manning provisions in the collective bargaining contract, but after mediation efforts and the report of an emergency board,[34] the national diesel agreement was accepted by the southern railroads in 1950. This arrangement, the same as the one previously in effect, remained in force until 1959 without raising any special difficulties. That year, however, the union complained that beginning in July, the Southern was not employing firemen on all trains. The railroad admitted the charge but replied that a shortage had resulted from vacation schedules. The position of the railroad during the negotiations which followed was that it is required by the diesel agreement to employ men only from among those on furlough, while the union said that additional men had to be hired regardless of whether any were on furlough. A strike to resolve the question was set by the union for July 26, 1960, but it was postponed during the mediatory attempts made by the National Mediation Board. The efforts of the NMB failed, and it terminated its jurisdiction in the case on June 4, 1962.

Meanwhile, on September 16, 1960, the Southern Railway Company, acting independently of the other carriers, served a notice on the unions proposing new rules defining the composition and size of train crews under which firemen would be eliminated by attrition. Then, on October 17, 1960, Southern withdrew from the negotiations being conducted under the nationwide notice of November 2, 1959. This dispute also went to the NMB.

On January 14, 1963, the Southern and seven of its subsidiary railroad companies, constituting the Southern Railway System, operating more than 7,000 miles of railroad, submitted the controversy over interpretation of the diesel agreement's requirement for employment of firemen to the National Railroad Adjustment Board for adjudication.

Shortly before, however, on September 10, 1962, the locomotive firemen had asked the federal district court for an injunction to compel the railroads to operate trains with firemen. On May 14, 1963, the court issued an injunction ordering the railroads to return to the *status quo* existing prior to 1959 pending a determination of the proper interpretation of the disputed contract provision by the National Railroad Adjustment Board.[35] Firemen had to be employed on all trains, the court said, because the railroad could not act independently, in contravention of the Railway Labor Act, to interpret a provision of the contract.

But the union returned to court charging the railroad with contempt for willful violation of the court order by continuing to operate some trains without a fireman taken from the seniority list of the union. Instead, aged and feeble men had been found and employed. The court, however, refused to cite the railroad for contempt.

Aside from the Southern Railway, the only other railroad which took individual action in the dispute was the Florida East Coast Railway Company. This carrier had been struck by its nonoperating employees in January, 1963 in a controversy over wages. On April 2, it notified its operating employees that the railroad work-rules notice of November 2, 1959 was being put into effect the following day. (The firemen issue, however, was excluded because the Florida East Coast announced that it had reached an agreement on this matter with an association that represents firemen.) Four operating unions struck on April 5. Although the National Mediation Board contended that the Florida East Coast could not impose new work rules until the work of the emergency board just appointed had been completed and procedures under the Railway Labor Act had been exhausted, the railroad maintained that it had withdrawn from national negotiations on March 12.[36] Despite the strike involving nearly 2,000 workers, some trains continued to run. At the request of the Justice Department, on May 7 a federal district court ordered the Florida East Coast to withdraw its order imposing work-rules changes, since it was subject to the proceedings of the emergency board. The railroad complied, but the strike of the nonoperating employees continued.[37]

On July 2, soon after the report of the emergency board was made, the Florida East Coast again imposed its work-rules changes on the operating employees. Thereupon the members of the operating unions, who had been observing the picket lines of the nonoperating workers, resumed their own stoppage.[38] But on August 29, the Secretary of Labor and the chairman of the National Mediation Board notified the carrier that it was subject to the arbitration law and must rescind the changes in rules it had made. The railroad complied.[39] Once again the operating employees terminated their strike but continued to respect the picket lines of the nonoperating workers.

Pressures for partial or complete merger of the five railroad operating unions have been increasing. The heads of the unions are more favorably disposed toward amalgamation than officers of lower rank in the hierarchy who are fearful that consolidation would reduce the number of administrative and elective positions. Yet the decline in railroad employment and hence in union membership has been sharp. In 1963, the membership was about 103,600 in the trainmen's union, 47,000 in the firemen's union, 37,000 in the engineers' union, 20,000 in the conductors' union, and 12,000 in the switchmen's union.[40] The dues, as high as ten dollars a month, are considerably more than the amount paid by highly skilled workers in other unions. They are irksome to many members, especially since most of the money is used for salaries and other disbursements to union officials and staff employees, many of whom are occupied with cases pending under the grievance procedure of the Railway Labor Act.

Merger may reduce operating costs, arrest declining membership, eliminate interunion strife and jealousies, and improve the effectiveness of the brotherhoods in collective bargaining negotiations. The five unions have carefully guarded the interests and rights of the separate crafts and classes they represent. Each has feared greater success by the others in bargaining. But if protection is guaranteed to smaller groups, combination prospects are brighter.

Several unions have been favorably inclined to merger in the past. The firemen, whose numerical decline has been most rapid, are more disposed to join with other unions. The engineers, whose union is the wealthiest of the group, have been most reluctant to do so.

The struggle by unions to prevent the bargaining away of jobs is the most important and most difficult labor-management issue of the 1960's. Compulsory arbitration as the solution to displacement of men by machines began on the railroads, but it may well serve as a pattern in other cases—particularly where the industry is affected with the public interest.

Chapter V

FEATHERBEDDING: OTHER TRANSPORTATION WORKERS

The furor over featherbedding among the operating railroad employees focused more attention on the existence of this practice elsewhere. Other transportation workers have been engaged in makework. These include nonoperating railroad workers, maritime workers, harbor workers, longshoremen, teamsters, and airline employees. Each of these groups has its own peculiar problems.

NONOPERATING RAILROAD EMPLOYEES

The main featherbedding controversy in the railroad industry concerns operating employees, but other groups of workers are not free of makework practices. Railroad telegraphers and station agents, one of the groups of nonoperating employees, provide a good illustration. In this case, arbitration proceedings were necessary to terminate featherbedding.

Beginning on November 5, 1957, the Chicago and North Western Railway Company, one of the major lines in the industry, filed petitions with four state public utility commissions to reorganize its station operations and discontinue some stations where fulltime work was no longer available for telegraphers and station agents. The plan would have meant loss of employment for some members of the Order of Railroad Telegraphers. Although several state commis-

101

sions approved the plan, intervening developments complicated the situation.

When the railroad began operating about 100 years ago,
local traffic dependent on horse-drawn vehicles required
stations every seven to ten miles. Poor management led to
a deterioration of facilities and equipment and the development of outmoded and wasteful practices. The financial
position of the line was greatly weakened. This made it impossible to compete effectively with modernized railroads
and other forms of transportation. Competition gradually
took away much of the freight and passengers and greatly
reduced the workloads at many stations. Investigation disclosed that at the stations involved, the amount of work
varied from twelve minutes to two hours per day, the
average being fifty-nine minutes. All agents, however, received a full day's pay, which in some cases represented as
much as $300 an hour for time actually worked. Further-
more, since union rules require work to begin at 8:30
in the morning, freight trains sometimes passed stations at
hours when agents were not on duty.

A new group of company officers, in an effort to improve
conditions, proposed the plan whereby several hundred
agents would be eliminated without any curtailment of service to the public. Several weeks after the company proposal, the union notified the railroad that it wished to
negotiate a contract provision prohibiting discontinuance of
any position in existence except by agreement. The carrier
maintained that the proposal was not a proper subject for
collective bargaining. After a number of conferences and
the unsuccessful mediatory efforts of the National Mediation
Board, the union secured from its membership an almost
unanimous vote in favor of a strike. A strike was called for
August 21, 1958. On the preceding day, however, the company obtained a temporary restraining order against the
strike from a district court in Illinois by arguing that the
union demand was not a lawfully bargainable subject under
the Railway Labor Act. After a full hearing the court held
that the issue was bargainable and dismissed the complaint.

The strike was restrained, however, pending determination of the appeal. On March 13, 1959, the Seventh Circuit Court of Appeals reversed the lower court and granted a permanent injunction against the strike. On April 18, 1960, however, the United States Supreme Court reversed the Circuit Court.[1] It held that the case grew out of a labor dispute within the meaning of the Norris-LaGuardia Act, and federal courts could not permanently enjoin a strike. The union's efforts to negotiate about job security, it said, are not an attempt to usurp legitimate managerial prerogatives, but involve a bargainable issue under the Railway Labor Act.

The union was free to strike. Negotiations were resumed, but they were unsuccessful. In order to forestall a strike, President Kennedy appointed an emergency board on April 23, 1962. The main recommendations of the board, made on June 14, were: that the union withdraw its demand that jobs should be eliminated only by mutual agreement; that the railroad set up a comprehensive program of protection for employees to ease displacement effects, including severance pay, furlough allowances, moving expenses for those transferred, preferential employment for those laid off, and retraining programs; and that relief employees without sufficient seniority should be guaranteed forty hours of pay a week. The board also suggested that the question of monetary claims made by the 700 telegraphers who had lost their jobs since 1955 should be negotiated further.[2] Although the company accepted the report, the union did not make its position clear.

On August 30, 1962, the cooling-off period having faded into the background, the telegraphers struck the railroad. About 16,500 employees were affected directly and the economy of nine states in the Midwest served by the line underwent hardship. On September 17, President Kennedy proposed binding arbitration of the major issues based on the guidelines laid down by the emergency board. Both sides agreed to the procedure, and the strike ended on September 28. The neutral member of the arbitration panel was nominated by the President and then designated by the National Mediation Board.

On October 8, 1962, the decision was reached by the arbitrator.[3] He ruled that the railroad may dismiss telegraphers whose work it finds unnecessary, but must give them ninety-day notices of such intention. This solution was adopted and ended the controversy. A pattern emerged. Subsequently a job stabilization settlement under similar terms was made by the union with the New York Central Railroad Company on December 10, 1962.

Railroad clerks are a second group of nonoperating railroad employees who were involved in displacement controversies. A long dispute between the Brotherhood of Railway Clerks and the Southern Pacific Company involved automation. On September 22, 1958, the union served notice on the carrier that it wanted a welfare section added to the collective bargaining contract covering stabilization and security in employment. Efforts by the railroad to remain competitive in the transportation field required technological improvement and organizational change. Between 1957 and 1962, regular and relief positions assigned to the clerks' union had fallen by about 4,500, or almost forty percent while traffic in revenue ton-miles had increased almost twelve percent. On August 10, 1962, President Kennedy appointed an emergency board under the Railway Labor Act. It made its report on December 31. The board recommended a negotiated program that would produce a projected rate of natural departures from the work force based on death, retirement, dismissal for cause, and promotion equal to or exceeding the number of jobs abolished by automation. Subsequently, the union set a strike date. A restraining order was issued by a California court and then vacated by a federal district judge at the request of the company, when the union agreed to resume negotiations and provide a 72-hour notice before striking. A strike would have tied up freight and passenger traffic in seven states from Texas to Oregon and idled 11,000 members of the union and 49,000 other employees of the company. On

March 17 agreement was reached on the basic issue providing for a system of natural attrition. Union members displaced by technology will receive a maximum of seventy percent of their normal pay for a year and sixty percent for the following four years. The pact generally followed the recommendations made by the emergency board. At the suggestion of President Kennedy, the parties had already agreed to resolve the remaining issues, which were relatively less important, by arbitration. The arbitration award was handed down on March 24, 1963.[4]

MARITIME WORKERS

Like other sectors of transportation, the maritime industry, which provides about 48,000 seafaring jobs, has been subject to featherbedding. The problem here, however, has special distinctiveness, since part of the industry is in direct competition with foreign merchantmen. American shipping starts with a heavy disadvantage because ablebodied seamen on ships flying the American flag receive three to seven times the wages paid to persons with similar ratings employed on foreign vessels.[5] Other job classifications in the merchant marine show comparable rate differences. Costs added by makework practices make it even more difficult for the industry to compete.

Though maritime wages abroad constitute a relatively small fraction of those in the United States, productivity of both groups of seamen is about the same.[6] In order to continue operating, therefore, large sections of the American merchant marine must be subsidized by the federal government. Furthermore, shipbuilding costs in the United States are roughly twice those of foreign costs. It is clear that mechanization and automation which introduce labor-saving devices will tend to reduce the costs of the industry in this country to a greater extent.

An advisory study made for the Maritime Administration of the United States Department of Commerce suggested that it might be wise to give the Maritime Administration

power to set maximum as well as minimum manning scales
on ships and possibly maximum wage rates for crew members. At present, subsidized operators have little incentive
to invest in labor-saving devices or resist union demands
which increase crew costs.[7]

Some parts of the shipping industry are interested in
increasing the number of larger and faster ships to compete
successfully with aircraft and railroads for premium cargoes.
Mechanization has lagged behind. Labor is a heavy cost to
the shipowners, and, over union opposition, naval architects
have been experimenting with automation processes and
techniques applicable to the industry. "It has been estimated
that the 55-man crew which is generally specified . . . costs
an employer $551,000 in wages a year. Yet, from the stand-
point of engineering and design, it is fairly simple to reduce
this crew by at least half."[8] This also means less space and
money for crew quarters and more for cargo. The change
may be accomplished by consolidating engine room equipment and providing semiautomatic steering and navigation.
Further progress in reducing manning needs may be expected in the future by using programming computers on
ships that are fully automated.

In an attempt to lessen resistance by labor unions to
technological change on ships, two shipping subsidiaries of
the Bethlehem Steel Corporation offered four unions—the
Seafarers' International Union, the Marine Engineers' Beneficial Association, the International Organization of Masters,
Mates, and Pilots, and the American Radio Association—an
arrangement to protect employment opportunities. For every
job eliminated on an American ship, the companies would
provide two at American wages and working conditions
aboard ships they owned flying foreign flags. This, the companies feel, would enable them to continue operating both
American and foreign flag vessels profitably.[9] The unions,
however, have not been interested in pursuing this
approach farther.

In addition to the problems of technological change,
the maritime industry is fettered by makework practices.

Many of these take the form of requiring overtime pay. One of the worst examples is the donkey watch where overtime is paid to engine room employees on regular duty between 5 P.M. and 8 A.M. whenever the ship loads or discharges cargo between those hours. This practice, long confirmed in collective bargaining agreements, goes back to the time when these employees had to keep up steam for the donkey engines which worked the winches. Winches have been operated by electric motors for years, but though the employees have nothing to do, overtime pay continues in effect. Overtime is also paid to ship waiters temporarily shifted to the dining room of a different class of service from that to which they are normally assigned and to passenger ship stewards serving at cocktail parties even if the work takes place during regular duty hours.

In August, 1963, the American Merchant Marine Institute and the National Maritime Union negotiated a four-year extension of their contract, which now terminates on June 15, 1969, covering 39,000 non-officer seamen employed aboard deep sea passenger, dry cargo, and tanker vessels. The new contract stresses security. The union gave up two scheduled wage increases of two and a quarter percent each, due in 1963 and 1964, for improved pension provisions. Beginning in 1965, seamen may retire at any age after twenty years of service with a pension of $150 a month. Previously, the pension was $125 a month after twenty years of service, payable at age sixty-five. The president of the NMU said that such contract changes are necessary and beneficial as automation is developed in the industry. An automation fund will be set up in 1965. It is to be financed by contributions from shipowners and is designed to help absorb the impact of technological change. How the money will be used is to be determined by a joint management-labor committee. Since 1956, an employment security fund in the industry has been used to pay supplemental unemployment insurance and dismissal wages.

HARBOR WORKERS

Workers employed in harbors are closely linked to both the railroad and maritime industries. Manning problems have proved to be vexing issues in several situations in the New York harbor. The most difficult case involved the marine railroad workers employed by the carriers to operate steam-powered passenger ferries between New Jersey and New York and steam- and diesel-powered tugboats to move harbor freight destined for ocean transport or other sections of the port by towing scows, barges, lighters, and car floats among the marine terminal facilities along the shorelines. The volume of traffic carried by marine departments of the carriers has declined sharply during the past decade, in contrast to the growth of other modes of transportation in and around New York.

In a dispute which had its origin in 1959, unions representing the railroad marine workers demanded, among other things, a rule establishing a fixed composition of crews upon the vessels. The carriers submitted a counterproposal to have an unrestricted right to determine the number of marine employees to be used. When negotiations and mediation did not lead to agreement, the President appointed an emergency board under the Railway Labor Act.

The board reported on December 10, 1960.[10] It rejected contentions by the unions that the employees should be identified and treated as seamen. The board found the characteristics of employment comparable to those of railroad workers. Operations are essentially similar to those of a shoreside rather than offshore industry. Upon consideration, the board concluded that the composition of crews should be determined by the carriers subject to review by an impartial board of adjustment. Recommendations were also made regarding wages, welfare benefits, holidays, vacations, and separation pay.

The parties, however, did not find a basis for agreement. On January 10, 1961, 664 crewmen on railroad ferries and tugs, members of the New York Railroad Marine Harbor

Council, composed of units of the Seafarers' International Union, Marine Engineers' Beneficial Association, and International Organization of Masters, Mates, and Pilots, struck eleven railroads and terminal and switching companies operating in the harbor. Freight and passenger traffic was tied up. The main issue was the right of the railroads to abolish jobs which they consider unnecessary. Both sides refused to yield for fear of establishing a precedent that would influence the Presidential Railroad Commission which had just been set up. Additional difficulty resulted from differences in customary bargaining procedures. Railroads frequently have had governmental intervention, fact-finding, and arbitration, but the maritime unions have been strongly averse to the interjection of third parties.

The railroads wanted authority to cut the five-man crews on harbor tugs. They were willing to agree not to abolish jobs for at least sixteen months, but insisted that any new contract provide that unnecessary jobs could be eliminated if adequate protection is afforded displaced workers. Binding arbitration would be used to resolve union disagreement with the company. The unions wanted a job abolished only when its duties were eliminated by new technology or new methods of work.[11]

The strike ended on January 23, 1961, on the basis of recommendations made by Secretary of Labor Arthur J. Goldberg, New York State Governor Nelson A. Rockefeller, and New York City Mayor Robert F. Wagner, Jr. On the pivotal issue, both sides agreed to maintain the *status quo* until after the report of the Presidential Railroad Commission had been made. The Commission would then be reconstituted to consider the railroad marine workers' manning dispute. Essentially, therefore, the union position prevailed. Goldberg, who had just joined President Kennedy's cabinet, said: "We won't have many strikes any more over wages or fringe benefits, as we did in the past. I expect that all the major labor disputes of the next few years will be over . . . men fearful of being thrown out of work by constantly improving machines."[12]

The Railroad Marine Workers Commission did its work between February and June, 1962. The Commission of nine members included three representatives of the public, three of the carriers, and three of the unions. Mediation efforts by the public members to clarify and resolve the issues in dispute did not avail.

The three issues which the Commission had to resolve were the questions whether there was need for a third deckhand (a fifth member of the crew) and oiler on tugboats and whether the wheelsman should be reclassified as assistant captain on ferryboats. The Commission contended that unilateral determination by the carriers was not in order because questions of safety and workload require that employees should be given a voice in determining the manning scales. In its report submitted to the President on June 11, 1962, the Commission found that the third deckhand was not necessary for safe and efficient operation of tugboats and recommended his phased elimination.[13] The process of gradual reduction should incorporate monetary guarantees and reemployment preference. The Commission rejected the demand of the unions for employment of an oiler (a position which had just previously been eliminated from diesel-powered tugboats by collective bargaining agreement) and denied the request for reclassification of wheelsman. A very strong dissent to the report was submitted by the three representatives of the union.

During the first part of 1961 strikes concerning employment by two other groups of New York harbor workers were narrowly averted. A contract between the employers' association representing the companies operating tugs, self-propelled lighters, tankers, and barges and the tugboat local of the National Maritime Union, representing about 3,500 men employed on 375 harbor craft, other than marine equipment of the railroads, was signed, but only after the union withdrew a demand to increase from three to four the number of crews assigned to boats working around the clock.[14] A second dispute, which began in 1959 between the railroad carriers and a local of the International Long-shoremen's Association, concerned the assignment of about 768 lighter captains on scows, barges, and lighters operated by the railroads in the harbor to ferry cargo between railroad waterside terminals and steamship piers. It had required the intervention of an emergency board,[15] and ended only when the manning issue was postponed until such time as the report of the Presidential Railroad Commission had been made.[16] The federal government agreed to set up a third special Presidential Railroad Commission which would then examine the job assignment question of lighter personnel.

The railroads have sought to reorganize the costly lighterage operations. They propose that they should have the right to determine when and if a lighter captain should be used and authority to assign him to more than one boat during the same tour of duty. The union opposes changes which will reduce the number of jobs, contending that safe and efficient operations and a practice accepted by the carriers for many years require that assignment of the men should not be altered when technology and methods of operation remain the same. Under contracts prevailing in 1963, lighter captains are assigned to their vessels for eight hours a day and five days per week. Regularly assigned men cannot normally be shifted from one boat to another in the course of a day.

The Railroad Lighter Captains Commission appointed by the President consisted of three persons representing the public, the carriers, and the union. It began to function in March, 1962 and submitted its report on July 9, 1962.[17] The Commission found that flexibility of assignment was essential to reduce costly and inefficient operations detrimental to the well-being of the industry. It recommended that railroads should have the right to use a lighter captain at more than one work location, and on more than one boat, during one work tour. Mandatory retirement at sixty-five years of age and protection to others in relation to length of seniority were recommended. Once again, a forceful dis-

sent to the conclusions was filed by the labor member of the
Commission.

LONGSHOREMEN

In the process of moving goods, longshoremen ordinarily
engage in duties which bridge the gap between the functions of seamen and teamsters. The work consists of moving
cargo between the dock and the hatch of ships engaged in
foreign, intercoastal, and coastal trade. This work is performed mainly by gangs of men, although some persons not
attached to a gang, such as clerks, checkers, carpenters, and
extra laborers, also are utilized. Since most of the costs of
operating a vessel, other than fuel, continue to accumulate
during the period in which the vessel is docked, profits tend
to be larger if turnarounds are more rapid. Fluctuations in
the demand for longshore labor vary widely from day to day
because arrival and departure of ships and amount and
kind of cargo to be loaded or unloaded are irregular. Some
casual employment, therefore, has been a regular feature
of the industry.

There are two unions in the industry. The International
Longshoremen's Association (ILA), which bargains for
about 50,000 workers in ports along the Atlantic and Gulf
coasts, has had a history of corruption and racketeering.
The International Longshoremen's and Warehousemen's
Union (ILWU), which broke away from the ILA and joined
the CIO in the 1930's, bargains for about 60,000 workers, of
whom about 15,000 are longshoremen on the West Coast.
The ILA is affiliated with the AFL-CIO, but the ILWU is
now independent. Bargaining in the West is coastwide,
whereas in the East and on the Gulf agreements in each
port follow the pattern negotiated in the harbor of New
York.

During the past few years, several new and improved
devices and techniques have decreased the number of man-
hours of work needed to handle cargo. Substantial reduction in manpower requirements has occurred in those cases

where bulk handling has replaced hand operations. Commodities such as petroleum, wheat, sugar, wine, cement, coal, and paper pulp lend themselves to this method. For example, the Petri Wine tanker which previously required 1,080 man-shifts to load two and a half million gallons needs only fourteen man-shifts under the new methods.[18] Unitization, which avoids handling individual boxes and packages, has been gaining ground. Straps and glue have been used with great effectiveness to group individual items into larger units. Huge containers are loaded before they are brought to the dock. Special equipment to handle bulk and unitized cargo is constantly being improved. Better equipment to lift and stow general cargo is also being introduced. These developments all serve to curtail the need for longshore labor.

The longshoring industry on the West Coast succeeded in eliminating restrictive working rules.[19] Great bitterness between the Pacific Maritime Association, which represents the shipping interests, and the International Longshoremen's and Warehousemen's Union prevailed during the period between 1934, when employers first recognized the union, and 1948. Major and minor strikes occurred with frequency. Various rules were developed by the union to increase the amount of work and reduce the effort necessary to perform the job. The most important rules of this type provided that: Cargo had to touch the "skin of the dock" in most ports before any worker but a longshoreman could handle it. This in effect is a double handling rule because loaded pallet boards from trucks or ships first had to be unloaded onto the floor of the dock, then rebuilt before being transferred; load limits generally were set arbitrarily at 2,100 pounds per pallet, even when available equipment could handle much more; the size of the longshore gang, negotiated locally, frequently consisted of an excessive number of men. For example, the rules typically required eight men in the hold of a ship, of which four were at work at any in an eight-hour day, with overtime at time and a half after time while the other four, called "witnesses," rested. Thus,

six hours, each of the eight men received nine hours' pay
for four hours of work. The rules were justified and de-
fended by the union as a means of preventing speed-ups
and encouraging safe operations. Subsequent to the ninety-
five-day strike of 1948, new management leadership helped
to usher in an era of relative peace. Each side was well-
disposed to reduce its financial losses. Realization by the
union that the volume of work available to longshoremen
was declining and that operating procedures were being
modernized by employers led to a reappraisal of its policies.
High labor costs on the docks were responsible at least
in part for the shift in freight transport from coastal
and intercoastal water shipments to trucks and railroads.
In 1957 the union announced that it was prepared to
forgo the advantages of its restrictive rules and prohibitions of technological change in order to make the
industry more competitive and profitable on the condition that employers would permit longshoremen to share
in the gains. A union committee reported: "Our present
policy can be described as one of intermittent guerrilla
warfare directed against all changes which we anticipate will
reduce the need for men." [20] Modification of the policy, the
union felt, would be more beneficial to the membership.[21]
Harry R. Bridges, the president of the union, said to the
representative of the employers: "A union leader has a right
to fight for featherbedding until an employer sits down and
works out a scheme for taking care of the men. Try to
change the work rules and we'll call a strike. We'll hold
out for three months—four, if necessary. We'll cost you
maybe 70 million dollars. Why don't you take half of that
and put it in a fund to protect the men's jobs as you
mechanize? Why don't you share the savings?" [22] The problems were explored with the employers' association that year
and in 1958.

The labor contract negotiated in 1959 provided that for
the contract year of 1959-1960 employers were free to
mechanize without fear of restraint by the union, although
they could make no changes in work practices. During this

period a method was to be devised to measure man-hours saved under the new techniques to provide a basis for future sharing of the gains. Meanwhile, the employers agreed to pay $1,500,000 into a fund to provide a guaranteed annual wage and early retirement.

Stevedoring contractors, usually paid on a cost-plus basis by the steamship lines to whom they supply longshoremen, frequently were not averse to loose labor practices which raised costs. The shipping employers' association, however, instituted a program of conformance and performance in 1959 under which fines are imposed on contractors who allow violation of the union contract to take place. Furthermore, if a dispute causes employees to cease work on any ship, employers halt all longshoring work in the port until work is resumed and the grievance procedure in the contract is followed. The successful use of these two devices gave employers confidence that labor costs could be reduced.

During 1960, shippers abandoned their original notion of creating a program geared to share the gains of mechanization and elimination of restrictive rules in favor of one in which fixed sums would be set aside to improve the working conditions of union members. The 1960 agreement provided essentially that, subject to agreement that there is adequate protection for employees against unsafe practices, onerous work, and speed-ups, employers may introduce new techniques and mechanization devices without restriction, terminate the employment of those who are unnecessary, and reassign employees to provide a more efficient work force. Employers agreed to pay $5,000,000 each year for five and a half years, to July 1, 1966, into a jointly trusteed mechanization and modernization fund to provide a guaranteed income to workers. The worker's income was to be equivalent to the wages of a number of hours each week determined by the trustees, when loss of work results from greater efficiency of operations. The benefits also include earlier retirement, and a lump-sum payment upon retirement, disability, or death. Although the contract forecloses reconsideration of the fund until 1966, it permits annual reviews of wages and hours.

These provisions protect only the 15,000 Class A (or fully registered) longshoremen of the West Coast. They do not apply to the 1,500 Class B workers who may be used to fill jobs when Class A men are not available and the 10,000 casual workers who are used when Class B workers are insufficient. In 1960, Class B and casual employees accounted for sixteen percent of all man-hours worked.

It is clear that under the new arrangements, as productivity increases, the labor force of longshoremen can be stabilized at a level well below the 27,000 men now attached to the operations. Reduction of manpower needs for the industry enables some workers to shift elsewhere and favorably affects overall economic growth. Protection for those currently in the longshoremen work force is afforded by the annual shrinkage resulting from deaths, retirements, and dropouts, which has risen from four percent to eight percent a year. This rise is due in part to the contract provisions making retirement practicable at age sixty-two.[23] Further security against unemployment is possible through reduction in the hours of the daily work shift. But this approach, although not especially desirable, has been unnecessary because huge investments are required to mechanize, and employers have not moved as rapidly to buy equipment and alter ship structures as had been expected.

Since work sharing arrangements for Class A men are in effect, any displacement which occurs during the next few years will be among Class B men and casuals. Yet the fund provides benefits for Class A men only. No benefits for those most likely to be displaced under the program are included. Indeed, to the extent that the amount of work available to any Class B man is reduced below the number of hours necessary to maintain the medical coverage he now has, that benefit would be lost.

On both the West and East coasts there has been some overlap between the jurisdictional work claims of the longshoremen and the teamsters. For a time in March, 1961, it appeared that the agreement between shippers and the ILWU would not succeed because longshoremen refused to cross picket lines set up by teamsters who claimed the right to load, unload, and move cargo on the docks—work which the industry was trying to eliminate. But compromise eased the situation in Los Angeles and San Francisco.[24]

The agreement has led to vast changes on the waterfront. Resistance to new techniques has almost disappeared. In fact, Harry Bridges has been urging more rapid mechanization to secure the relief from heavy work called for by the pact. Reduction in work force has enabled employers to increase the wage rates between 1958 and 1962 without adding to total labor costs. But not only has unit labor cost fallen, more rapid loading and unloading of ships has reduced turnaround time. This enables vessels to be used for more loads. It is the equivalent of adding ships to the fleet without cost. Developing larger units of cargo by using pallets, cribs, containers, whalebacks, and vans has also reduced damage and pilferage losses.

Recent labor-management relations on the East and Gulf coasts have been in sharp contrast to those in the West. The work-rules problem has been a matter of grave concern and contention. The work gang of twenty men (twenty-one when the foreman is included) has been standard in the New York dock area for many years, although its size varies in other ports. The union objects to cargo which is containerized or prepalletized away from the piers, since such techniques may reduce the size of the gang necessary to load and unload ships. The greatest difficulty in resolving problems on the East Coast has resulted from the failure of the parties to develop a disposition to agree.

Although the ILA and longshoremen fear that rapid changes in work methods and mechanization in the future will cause serious displacement of labor, this problem has not arisen during the past decade. While the total longshore work force has been shrinking in the Port of New York under the rules set forth by the bistate Waterfront Commission, the number of man-hours of work available has not changed significantly.[25] The union has fought hard against new devices and techniques which increase the speed at which work can be done and against all efforts to reduce the size of the gang. In 1959, however, agreements were reached to set up a container fund and a bulk sugar fund.

Employers find that containerization, a form of unitization, reduces packing and handling requirements, lessens theft and damage, and lowers insurance costs. The work of longshoremen is sharply reduced even if the container is loaded on the dock because of the time saved in lifting and stowing the cargo. As the volume of goods shipped in containers rose sharply in the late 1950's, the ILA made several efforts in the New York area to stop handling them. Arbitration and negotiation led to agreement that royalties on containers loaded or unloaded away from the pier by non-ILA labor would be paid into a jointly administered trust fund. The amount of payment was later fixed by arbitration and is higher for vessels which are more automated. Although royalty charges thus far have not been large enough to deter containerization, by 1962 less than five percent of all cargo in the port was carried by container. Employers were given the right to use all types of containers without restriction by the union, but they have agreed that they would retain the twenty-man gang on all container operations and would not subcontract loading or unloading containers to employers whose workers are not members of the ILA.

The sugar companies with refining facilities in the New York area gradually converted their operations from general to bulk cargo during the 1950's. Unbagged raw sugar moved by special equipment, requiring much less labor, replaced the bags of sugar. The 1959 bulk sugar fund agreement fixed a royalty to be paid into a jointly administered fund which is used to provide additional medical benefits for members of the Brooklyn Local of the ILA in whose jurisdiction the unloading occurs. The major concession made by the union on this occasion has been to permit the size of the gang on sugar operations to be cut to nine men. But the fund provides no displacement benefits.

The displacement fears of the East Coast longshoremen were expressed by the president of the Brooklyn Local in a report to the membership.[26] He illustrated how machinery may rid the factories and piers of workers. In 1956, he wrote, just before the National Sugar Refining Company began automating its Long Island City Jack Frost operation, each ship was worked by seventy men, consisting of three gangs of twenty-three employees and a shop steward. In addition, seventy-five warehousemen worked in the sugar house receiving the product and several coopers worked on the piers mending bags. In 1963, under the agreement, automated sugar ships are worked by thirty-three longshoremen divided into two flexible gangs. The inside warehousemen are no longer necessary and, since the sugar is now loose rather than bagged, coopers are not used. Prior to 1956, seventy men unloaded about 180 tons of bagged sugar an hour. In 1963, thirty-three men remove 450 tons of loose sugar in the same period of time. Ships which formerly required five days to turn around now do so in two. Employment has fallen as fewer men unload ships much more rapidly.

The International Longshoremen's Association and the New York Shipping Association negotiated a three-year contract in 1959 only after a week-long strike had occurred. The contract sets the pattern for the other East and Gulf coasts ports. Longshoremen receive straight-time pay for eight hours of work between 8 A.M. to noon and 1 P.M. to 5 P.M. and are guaranteed four hours of pay on any day that they are called to work. It was clear after prolonged bargaining in 1962 that the union was not prepared to compromise on demands by employers for a reduction in the size of the twenty-man gang and greater flexibility in assigning men in order to improve cargo handling on the piers. Employers charged featherbedding. They wanted gangs to consist of six to sixteen men, depending on the type of cargo handled. Employers complained that productivity declined because work rules have frozen the assignment of gangs. Of the twenty men in the gang, usually eight are in the hold, four on the deck, and eight on the dock. Employers contend that often half the men on the dock have no work and should be in the hold.

The ILA maintains that proposed changes would eliminate 6,000 of the 26,000 jobs in the Port of New York alone. Thomas W. Gleason, general organizer of the union said: "It has taken years and all sorts of fights and Presidential commissions to get one fireman out of a diesel cab and one flight engineer out of a cockpit, and they haven't done it yet. And these operators think they can throw four or twelve men out of a work gang just like that!" [27] The ILA contends that the size of the work gang was not an important issue on the West Coast. Longshoremen there, under a system of rotary hiring, ordinarily worked with different individuals on different-sized gangs. On the East Coast, the gang is often a fixed social, political, and work unit.

Wage issues also separated the parties, but these were of lesser importance. After fifteen weeks of almost fruitless negotiations, 52,000 longshoremen struck the ports from Maine to Texas when the contract expired on October 1. President Kennedy appointed an emergency board under the Taft-Hartley Act, and an injunction barring the strike for eighty days was obtained on October 4. The emergency board stepped out of the dispute on October 31 after declaring that the situation appeared insoluble. The Federal Mediation and Conciliation Service took over efforts to bring the parties together. Both the Mediation Service and Secretary of Labor Wirtz, who also intervened, failed. Upon expiration of the injunction on December 23, the ILA resumed the strike.

With economic losses to the nation running at the rate of millions of dollars a day, according to President Kennedy, he appointed a special three-man board, headed by Senator Morse on January 16, 1963, to mediate a settlement, or failing that, to recommend a procedure for ending the strike. The board made wage recommendations which were accepted by both sides, although reluctantly by management, and the strike ended on January 25. However, the featherbedding question already had been set aside by the disputants. Upon suggestion of the federal government, both sides agreed prior to the resumption of the strike in December, that a manpower utilization and job security study of the industry would be made under the direction of the Secretary of Labor. Future bargaining will be based upon the results of this study. But by the time this agreement had been reached, bitterness between employers and the union was so intense that the wage issue could not be considered calmly, and the strike had been reactivated.

The fifteen-month study of manpower utilization by the Department of Labor will deal with job security, automation, severance pay, work force flexibility, gang size, closing of eligible work registers used for hiring, and other facets. Under the agreement between the parties, results of the study will be used for purposes of negotiating the new contract. If no accord is achieved at least two months before the expiration of the present two-year contract on September 30, 1964, the parties will name neutral members to a body to make nonbinding recommendations.

TEAMSTERS

The trucking industry has not been free from featherbedding, but the practices are few and the problems are minor compared to those on the railroads. The cost impact of certain labor practices in the industry, however, has become more significant as railroads, in efforts to increase the share of freight which they haul, have tended to reduce cargo rates while trucking companies have been forced to raise theirs.[28] But unlike the railroad industry, trucking companies have refrained from publicizing any featherbedding problems which they have. This policy stems from the notion that calm collective bargaining negotiations with the teamsters' union is likely to be more fruitful in bringing about elimination of undesirable practices than heated and bitter controversy. For example, the union agreed in the central states contract negotiated in the mid-1950's to permit truck operators to replace the mileage tables in effect and pay drivers for mileage actually driven when new highways had substantially reduced road distances between some cities.[29] It was a union concession which recognized competitive pressures and employment problems. In the New York area, contractual provisions requiring an employee to be used in accordance with strict work classification schedules were modified to permit him to work at different jobs provided his compensation is at the highest rate for the work performed. This change was particularly beneficial to small employers whose volume of business makes it too costly to use different employees in each classification. Truckers also realize that controversy with the local union is likely to bring immediate and costly retaliation in the day-to-day enforcement of contract provisions. The relative strength of the union in this industry, where the typical employer is small, is much greater than it is on the railroads.

A spokesman for the trucking industry has said: "You have just got to give [James R.] Hoffa [president of the teamsters' union] credit for buying the idea that the industry will pay well for work done but must stop paying for work not done."[30] In eliminating some of the featherbedding practices, the carriers and union have followed a policy under which wage payments to workers affected are not reduced. Instead, increases are not granted or are smaller until the desired adjustment has been made. For example, when trip rates in New England became unduly high, drivers on those runs did not receive wage increases when hourly and mileage rates were raised.

Nevertheless, there are many makework practices in the trucking industry similar to those on the railroads. They are, however, generally confined to limited geographical areas. Work of local drivers is protected when it would be far less costly to have road drivers do the job. Trucking company employees are sometimes paid for the time it would take them to unload trucks even when shipping company employees do all the work. A guaranteed minimum number of paid hours for short runs, extra pay for delay in notification of assignments, use of unnecessary helpers on local delivery trucks, and paid waiting time or "baby-sitting" when the truck is loaded or unloaded are isolated practices which add significant labor costs where they are found.

The teamsters have been faced by new methods of operation and types of equipment which have tended to displace truck drivers. Although the union does not ordinarily oppose technological change, there have been occasions when it has resisted innovation or attempted to make its use economically burdensome to employers. An important area of conflict has been piggyback operations.

Piggybacking transportation began in 1926, but substantial use of this device did not occur until the 1950's. It reduces the volume of work done by over-the-road truck drivers because railroads, rather than trucking companies, carry the trailer between the cities of origin and destination. Similar displacement problems arise in fishyback, barge, and birdyback operations. An agreement between the teamsters' union and the trucking companies in the Midwest in 1961 provided that, effective in 1962, a royalty of five dollars would be paid into the pension or health and welfare fund for all trailers shipped by piggyback, fishyback, barge, or birdyback.[31] Similar provisions were subsequently incorporated in contracts covering most of the rest of the country.

The tax imposed by the union to discourage the use of piggybacking did not please the trucking companies, railroads, or railroad unions. The teamsters' union maintains that royalties used to increase the pension fund would enable truck drivers to retire at an earlier age, but there have been several obstacles to the implementation of the agreement. The provision is difficult to police, and the union has shown some indecision about collecting payments. Many truck operators are indisposed to pay the levy.[32] More important, in mid-1963, there were thirteen states which made it illegal, imposing stiff penalties, for a motor carrier to pay a fee to a union for sending its trailers by another mode of transportation. The constitutionality of these laws, however, is doubtful since there is often a question as to whether states may deal with interstate commerce matters. There are almost no wholly intrastate piggyback operations. Thus the question of piggyback operations remains unsettled.

LOCAL TRANSIT WORKERS

The matter of converting bus and trolley crews from two men to one man involved much friction over a number of years, but generally management was successful in making the change. Conversion was accomplished by unilateral decision, collective bargaining agreements with the union, arbitration awards, or court authorization. Much of the unsuccessful struggle against technological displacement was waged by the street and electric railway employees' union.

The first horse-drawn cars used only one employee who both drove the car and served as conductor. When electricity was introduced and vehicles became larger a second man was usually added. Soon thereafter, as improved designs and new safety devices became standard equipment, companies tried to reduce the crew to one man. Generally, the early efforts by management, beginning at the end of the nineteenth century, were unsuccessful. During World War I and immediately thereafter, however, labor was scarce and new safety devices and other equipment for one-man operation were further substantially improved. Union resistance eased a little, and some progress was made by management. When the union renewed its campaign against one-man crews in the early 1920's, emphasizing that trolley cars and buses with one-man crews were susceptible to more accidents and holdups, it succeeded only in obtaining a differential rate of pay for operators of one-man cars.[33] The policy of the union vacillated because its officials were torn between knowledge that much previous resistance by labor to technological advance had failed and the evidence of displacement which was apparent. Nevertheless the second man was gradually eliminated in public local transportation over the next quarter of a century.

An ordinance in the city of Shreveport, Louisiana, requiring two men to operate streetcars was declared unconstitutional by a federal circuit court in 1930 even though an earlier decision by the United States Supreme Court had upheld the law. The circuit court said that conditions had sufficiently changed in the interim to render the ordinance unreasonable and unnecessary and its enforcement confiscatory.[34] The Fifth Avenue Coach Company in New York City, in dire financial straits in 1946, was permitted by an arbitrator to reduce its bus crews from two men to one man.[35] It was one of the last carriers using two-man operations. In 1948, the New York City Transit Authority was authorized by an arbitrator to use one conductor on each train in place of the two formerly used. In this case, permanent employees did not lose their jobs.[36]

AIRLINE EMPLOYEES

The first commercial flights, mainly engaged to carry mail, were manned by crews consisting of a single pilot. Expansion into the passenger business on a more widespread and regular basis during the 1930's resulted in the addition of a second pilot. At present two men still constitute the crew complement of planes weighing less than 80,000 pounds. A flight engineer, the third member of the crew, was first used on domestic flights of stratoplanes in 1939. During World War II a mechanic was placed aboard many air contract carriers engaged in oceanic flights. Lack of adequate personnel and facilities in many places required that a man who could make or supervise repairs should be taken along.

Almost from the beginning, employees in the airline industry were plagued by fears of technological displacement. They resisted when the carriers decided early in the 1930's to alter the traditional method of computing the wages of pilots, based on mileage flown, by instituting a system under which the hours of work would constitute the important element. The problem was brought before the National Labor Board which found that: "The Industry is on the threshold of technological improvement which will greatly accelerate the speed of airplane travel and which may result in some technological unemployment." [37] On the principle that both sides should share in the benefits of technological advance, the Board devised a formula limiting the hours of work to eighty-five and using both the number of miles flown, under which pilots derive the advantages of technical progress, and hours worked, under which the airlines do, as factors in determining wages. This complicated structure, created in 1934 and subsequently implemented by federal legislation, has remained the minimum level of pay for pilots to the present day.

During the succeeding years, conflicting interests among aircraft manufacturers, airline companies, unions, government agencies, and the public were apparent. Although the matter of safe operation of the plane was always in the forefront of the discussion and debate, economic and political considerations relating to profits and industrial peace were never wholly absent.

As a result of an increasing number of commercial airplane accidents, a special board of inquiry appointed by President Harry S. Truman in 1947 recommended that the Civil Aeronautics Board should conduct hearings to determine whether more than two men were needed in the cockpit. In 1948, the CAB decided that aircraft with a takeoff weight of more than 80,000 pounds would be required to include a third crew member to be used "solely as a flight engineer" to perform certain mechanical duties and enable pilots to concentrate on critical flight instruments and controls. The objection of several carriers to the limitation imposed on the duties of the flight engineer led to a deletion of the restriction on the functions of the third man in the final draft of the CAB regulations.[38]

Two distinct methods were used by the industry to implement the 1948 regulation. A majority of the larger airlines followed the practice of employing persons with a mechanical background as flight engineers. He was not required to have training as a pilot; he was engaged in monitoring and adjusting the system units. The other air carriers assigned the third seat to pilots who also held certificates as flight engineers. This enabled the engineer to interchange duties with other members of the crew. Under this pattern of development, the first group of companies recognize flight engineers as a separate craft, represented for bargaining purposes by a union distinct from the one which negotiates for pilots. On the other lines, the entire crew on the flight deck is considered one class and is represented by a union of pilots. The safety records of both groups of airlines have been equally good.[39]

Changing technology in the air transport industry, which in the past decade has been marked by the introduction of jet planes, has intensified some of the prevalent labor problems. The renewal of bitter strife in the industry and the development of featherbedding arrangements did not occur until the introduction of jet turbine-powered aircraft became imminent. These passenger aircraft, introduced in 1959, can do more work than fifteen of the type used in the middle of the 1930's. Rapid increases in productivity and alterations in technique have highlighted those problems of flight personnel concerned with qualifications, training, job security, future employment opportunities, and collective bargaining representation.

The first case, which required the National Mediation Board to determine the composition of the appropriate craft or class of flight deck or cockpit crew members in the airline industry for purposes of representation, provided the setting for a thorough airing of the role of the aircraft flight engineer. It also opened up the matter of featherbedding on the airlines. This case arose in 1959 when the Air Line Pilots Association (ALPA) filed a petition alleging the existence of a representation dispute at United Air Lines. Prior to that time the Board had been involved only in determining which union should represent a group whose composition previously had been agreed to by the parties. Unlike railroad cases coming before the NMB, where craft and class lines had already crystallized, the situation in the much newer air carrier industry was still marked by a considerable degree of fluidity caused by the impact of government regulation, collective bargaining, policies of individual companies, differences in equipment used, and rapid technological change.

After investigating the case thoroughly, using the assistance of an outside committee of neutrals, the NMB decided on January 17, 1961 that the pilot, copilot, and flight engineer constitute one craft or class at United Air Lines for purposes of representation and collective bargaining under the Railway Labor Act and should vote as a single unit.[40] This development precipitated a strike by members of the Flight Engineers' International Association (FEIA) at seven of the nation's air carriers on February 17, 1961. The carriers were American Airlines, Eastern Air Lines, National Airlines, Pan American World Airways, Flying Tiger Line, Trans World Airlines, and Western Airlines. The flight engineers feared the ALPA would file petitions and ultimately, because of its numerical preponderance, win elections for the establishment of a single craft or class at carriers other than United Air Lines. The controversy was complicated by the curious composition of flight deck crews on jet planes.

On February 21, 1961, upon recommendation of Secretary of Labor Goldberg, President Kennedy issued Executive Order 10921, supplemented two days later by Executive Order 10922, which established a commission to examine the issues in the controversy, to report its findings and recommendations to the President, and to assist the parties in achieving an amicable settlement. The issues involved differences regarding the functions of the flight engineers, the job security of flight engineers, and the representation rights of the ALPA and the FEIA.

The controversy between the ALPA and the FEIA concerning the third member of the crew, who by regulations of the Federal Aviation Agency must have a flight engineer's certificate, was an important matter facing the commission. It involved piston and jet aircraft. Both unions agreed that two occupants of the cockpit should be pilots, but insisted that the third man should have higher qualification than those specified by the FAA. Using safety as its basis, the FEIA contended that the third person should be a mechanical specialist who knows the highly complex structure of the plane and who holds a mechanic's certificate with airframe and powerplant ratings (A and P license). The ALPA argued that the simplification of systems and reduction of mechanical duties, particularly on jets, make it more desirable that all three flight crew members should be qualified pilots. Both job control and security underlie the position of each union. The FEIA maintains that the ALPA is trying to gain the flight engineer's seat for pilots, while the ALPA argues that distinct crafts in the cockpit represented by different unions are no longer justified. The carriers have been caught in the midst of the conflict. They proposed that the third man in the crew hold either a commercial pilot's certificate or a flight engineer's certificate and that his primary duty during flight should be to assist the pilot in command.

Although an emergency board in the Eastern Air Lines case recommended in July, 1958 that flight engineers serving on turbojet planes should be licensed pilots,[41] a strike and other pressure by the FEIA on the air carriers led to a number of collective bargaining agreements in the industry. These agreements specified that requirements for the third seat would include a flight engineer's certificate but not pilot qualifications. However, the mandatory policy formulated by the ALPA at its 1958 convention, that three flight stations on jet planes should be manned by qualified pilots, appeared to block the introduction of jet planes in commercial service. In order to use the jet planes, the delivery of which was beginning, some of the carriers compromised. They agreed to employ a fourth person in the turbojet cockpit. Three members of the flight deck were pilots and

the fourth was a flight engineer who needed no training as
a pilot.

The result was that lines flying the same routes and using
similar equipment operated with different crew complements
and qualifications. A few lines used crews of four. Those
which had three men in the crew (generally carriers bargaining only with the ALPA) required in some cases that
all should be licensed pilots, but that at least one man
have a flight engineer's certificate; in other cases they required that the third seat should be held by a person with
a background either as a pilot only or both as a mechanic
and a pilot. Equipment interchange led to situations where
one leg of a flight required a crew of three and another part
of the same run used a crew of four.

The Presidential Commission, which reported on May
24, 1961, found that safe and efficient operation of jet aircraft requires a crew of three.[42] It reported that based on
an evaluation of interchangeability of functions, efficiency,
and job security, a crew of three pilots is most advantageous.
The Commission said that the fourth man constituted a
featherbedding cost for which the carriers were responsible
at least in part, because they had failed to exercise proper
judgment and had adopted expedient solutions instead. The
Commission recommended a gradual transition from four
men to three in those cases where a fourth man was in the
crew, but with adequate protection of job equities. This
was to be afforded by the operation of normal attrition and
the availability of severance pay, early retirement, and suitable ground jobs. The Commission felt that the ultimate
solution to the representation conflict between the unions
lies in a merger of the two on a fair basis with adequate
legal safeguards for the interests of the flight engineers.
Indeed, it pointed out that in 1958 the executive council of
the AFL-CIO had adopted a report of one of its subcommittees which stated that the ALPA and the FEIA would
benefit from a merger. The Commission spelled out its
recommendations in great detail in a supplemental report
issued on October 17, 1961.

Management contended that the use of a fourth man in the crew of jets had unnecessarily increased the operating costs of the airline industry during the three years between 1959 and 1962 by $25,000,000 to $30,000,000.[43] Nevertheless, the larger companies and the two unions made little progress in resolving the deadlock. Attempts to negotiate new contracts were not immediately successful despite recognition by union leadership that the fourth man in the crew is unnecessary. The president of the FEIA wrote that the fourth man in the cockpit of jets "is probably the most glaring example of 'make-work' that has come into being since the industrial revolution . . . . he contributes absolutely nothing to the safety or efficiency of the flight." [44] But as a result of intricate negotiations involving the companies and unions, mediation, the work of four more emergency boards,[45] arbitration proceedings, strikes, and court interventions, the four carriers using four-man crews on jets—American Airlines, Eastern Air Lines, Pan American World Airways, and Trans World Airlines—were able to reduce the number of men in the cockpit from four to three in 1962 and 1963. Complete agreement was reached between both unions and Trans World Airlines. Attrition of flight engineers and severance pay for those who do not wish to complete a specified amount of pilot training are among the basic elements in the solution. Assurances were provided by representatives of the federal government, as suggested by the Presidential Commission, that for some unspecified period of time the rights of the FEIA to represent flight engineers would not be prejudiced by the new collective bargaining agreement. Eastern and Pan American worked out arrangements with the ALPA. The former carrier cut the number of men in the cockpit at the cost of a strike by the flight engineers;[46] the latter reduced the size of the crew despite legal protests by the FEIA.[47]

Pilots of American Airlines, who constituted more than a tenth of the ALPA membership, decided to break away from the Association and form an independent union, the Allied Pilots Association. The issue in dispute concerned

qualifications of the third pilot on jet planes. The ALPA
wants him to hold a commercial and instrument pilot rating,
while the rebel group feels that the minimum pilot license,
which would enable the third man to take over in an
emergency, is sufficient.[48]

The ALPA tried unsuccessfully to block the establishment
of the Allied Pilots Association.[49] On July 9, 1963, however,
American Airlines signed a two-year contract with the new
union after being shown proof that a majority of its pilots
and copilots had designated the new group as the bargaining representative. The status of the flight engineers' union
at American is in doubt.[50]

Thus not only has the merger problem between pilots
and flight engineers remained unsolved, but the internecine
struggle among pilots has added complications. It is clear
that the crews on all jet planes will be reduced to three
men, but resolution of the merger issue and final determination of the qualifications for the third man have not been
worked out. Settlement of these matters has been particularly difficult at American Airlines. Though the featherbedding situation which for a time had existed in the
cockpit of the jet planes has been cleared up, it may
emerge again unless effective consolidation of the three
unions takes place soon.

Chapter VI

FEATHERBEDDING: INDUSTRIES OTHER THAN TRANSPORTATION

Aside from the transportation industry, featherbedding is practiced widely only in construction, entertainment, and printing. Elsewhere in the economy, formal union rules do not provide for restriction of output or resistance to technological advance. Some obsolete rules, particularly in certain sectors of manufacturing, need revision and modernization, but these do not generally concern makework deliberately imposed or supported by the union.

CONSTRUCTION

Some of the most flagrant and persistent cases of featherbedding have occurred in the construction industry. Many varied illustrations of mid-nineteenth-century practices were given by economist William T. Thornton, writing 100 years ago. He noted that many unions really mean making work when they talk of doing work. Unionists seek to obtain the highest possible wages in return for the least possible work, and try to do that little with the least possible inconvenience to themselves. Building trades workers are condemned for extravagant work rules requiring excessively minute division of labor, limiting ordinary activity of movement, and preventing material used in one area from being manufactured in another.[1]

Unions in the building trades have continued to resist technological advance vigorously and, on the whole, successfully to the present day. Opposition has been directed

133

at changes affecting employment opportunities adversely or reducing the need for acquired skills.

Several factors make it possible for building trades unions to resist effectively. In the first place, though the effect of a restriction on a particular work operation may be great, the total cost of a building ordinarily increases only slightly. Consequently, employers are not willing to undergo great expense or fight hard to bar the restriction. Secondly, union resistance to technology affects only a small part of the work of each of the skilled craftsmen, and employers need these men to perform other duties and functions. Thirdly, nonunion competition rarely exists because unions have been ordinarily able to organize all employers involved within geographically competitive areas. Alternative labor sources are not, therefore, available to employers. A fourth consideration is that the different unions involved have supported each other and have reduced the ability of employers to counteract demands. Fifthly, construction is often subject to time commitments, and builders avoid delay whenever possible because it is costly.

In different places and at different times, attempts have been made to eliminate restrictions on output and machinery by building trades workers. Often the efforts are successful for short periods, but the agreements reached for such purposes have not usually been enduring. Generally, the struggle has followed recurring phases. Restrictive union rules have eased when pressures by employers have increased, governmental investigations have been made, adverse business conditions have prevailed, or nonunion competition has been strong.

Featherbedding in the construction industry occurs because of the uncertainties of employment. The fact that work typically is not steady has induced unions to formulate rules prolonging tasks and resisting changes which would further shorten the length of time required to do a job. Union rules have been designed to maintain the handicraft character of building operations, localize the market, decentralize production, and require unnecessary development and refinement of the product. A comprehensive scholarly study made more than a quarter of a century ago revealed many practices in the building trades intended to make work.[2]

Makework situations in the building trades are lent countenance by collective bargaining agreements, occasional legal enactments, or unilateral union decisions which set maximum daily work quotas or require time-consuming methods of work for carpenters, painters, bricklayers, electricians, and other skilled construction workers.[3] Painters sometimes fix the square feet of surface they paint, limit the width of the brush, or use brushes where sprayers are more efficient. Quotas may be set on the number of bricks which masons place in a day. Carpenters may object to the use of prefabricated panels and require the work to be done at the construction site. Electricians may refuse to install wiring work done in the factory or shop. In some areas, plumbers have refused to use pipe threaded at the place of manufacture. Undue emphasis on quality also causes a reduction in output. Specialization of work in the industry is occasionally excessive and becomes very burdensome for small contractors.

The featherbedding problem is more acute on smaller construction jobs, such as private home building. In part this arises because collective bargaining agreements frequently are negotiated between locals and the largest contractors, businessmen involved primarily in constructing office buildings, large apartment houses, roads, and public works rather than small homes. These employers are more willing and able to accept demands and rules calling for a high degree of division of labor and specifying that particular workers must perform certain tasks. They can agree to this because they employ many workers who do the same operation on each building project. Nevertheless, large employers also find featherbedding costs burdensome as concessions accumulate. Another factor which bears on restrictive practices is the large amount of subcontracting practiced in the industry which divides responsibility and control.

The emphasis which unions in the building trades put on maintaining standards of quality, not always justified, tends to restrict output. Efforts may be directed at enforcing provisions in the municipal building code, the fire underwriters' code, a contract between the owner of the building and the contractor, or rules promulgated by the local unions. Unions, however, have not been as alert to their interests as might be expected when employers have tended to neglect different specification requirements which would lead to the utilization of more labor. "In fact, rules requiring the observance of specifications and codes have probably been more important as sources of graft to union officials than as sources of employment to union members." [4]

It has been suggested that city building codes, which limit the use of new construction materials and processes, as for example those requiring plaster walls when they are no longer necessary to meet fire-safety standards, may be the product of pressures from businessmen who have vested interests at stake rather than unions which seek more work. Some union officials have contended that a small cut in interest rates in the building industry would be a much more effective way of reducing the cost of homes than any changes in the codes. Nevertheless, independent action is possible in respect to each of these matters.

On numerous occasions during the twentieth century, featherbedding practices in the construction industry have been brought to the sharp attention of the public. Investigation of the Chicago labor disputes of 1900 by the United States Industrial Commission disclosed that several unions in the building trades, including plumbers, gas fitters, lathers, and carpenters, had set formal and specific restrictions on the amount of work which might be performed in a day. The employers objected throughout duration of the dispute to union restrictions on output, and provisions in the contracts which settled the controversy prohibited such

practices in the future.[5] Clearly, the agreements were ineffective in this respect.

A legislative investigation of housing problems in New
York, under the chairmanship of Charles C. Lockwood of
the New York State Senate, which began in 1919 and
terminated with a final report at the end of 1922 disclosed
flagrant union restrictions of output in the building trades.
The Lockwood Committee was concerned with many facets
of the housing shortages which marked that period. With
respect to labor, it said: "The Committee is satisfied that
if organized labor in the building industry removes the
restrictions and abuses . . . there would soon be a supply
of labor in the State sufficient to meet the demand."[6] The
Committee revealed that labor unions were responsible for
the existence of many unfair practices and regulations in the
building trades which destroyed efficiency, delayed operations, and increased expenses. Such practices included, for
example, destruction of molds and models after they had
once been used even though they might be useful again;
prohibition of labor-saving devices and machinery approved
by public authorities; requirements that work which could
be performed in the shop more cheaply should be done on
the job at greater expense; and the removal of ornamental
construction because it is not up to the artistic standards of
union delegates although acceptable to the architects and
owners.[7]

The Committee criticized a local of the plasterers' union
in New York City which insisted on furnishing three, rather
than two, coats of plaster for one and two family houses
in order to provide more work for its members. Such unnecessary work increased the cost of each house by approxi-
mately $110.[8] The Committee did not propose legislation
to correct abuses. It felt that the unions should be allowed
more time to modify their behavior along lines recommended.

In October, 1922 an agreement in New York City between
the building trades employers' association representing employers and the building trades council representing unions

set forth a group of twelve principles as the basis of union
contracts in the construction industry. The third of these
principles bears on featherbedding. It specified that neither
the amount of work a man may perform nor the use of
machinery, tools, appliances, or methods shall be restricted
or interfered with by a union or its officers.[9]

Wide variation in the work performance of the different
building crafts has been common. A pioneering study made
by the Bureau of Labor Statistics of the United States Department of Labor in 1923 showed that bricklaying in
straightaway walls ranged from 95.7 bricks per hour in
Indianapolis to 241.0 bricks per hour in Birmingham. The
number of square yards plastered per man-hour varied
between 4.5 in Boston and 7.8 in Philadelphia.[10]

Opposition to the introduction of new devices and techniques by building trades continued throughout the 1930's
and 1940's. Divergent views regarding restrictions were expressed by two investigators who studied the housing problems for two different Congressional committees in the
postwar period. Senator Joseph R. McCarthy reported to
the Joint Committee on Housing on the basis of hearings
and informal conferences conducted in practically every
major city in the United States, that generally most of the
blame for the postwar housing shortage was placed on
labor. He indicated, however, that though labor was guilty
of some abuses, the criticism appeared unduly excessive.
"As for the cost factor, labor still represents about the
same proportion of the total construction cost as it did in
prewar years. The decreased productivity in the building
trades would appear to be no greater than in any other
line of work. People simply are not working as hard or as
long hours as they did during the war years, and the contrast is noticeable everywhere. The decreased productivity
in the building industry is particularly exaggerated, for
building workers today are working under entirely different
conditions than in prewar years."[11] McCarthy illustrated
with the testimony of a typical bricklayer who admitted that
he laid only 250 bricks a day in contrast to 2,000 in previous

years, but who said that the work was nevertheless harder because it involved a brick-veneer building in contrast to a solid brick wall. Senator McCarthy added that part of the decline in productivity was due to the increased age of the skilled building trades workers.

At the beginning of 1948, the chairman of the Joint Committee on Housing in Congress announced that the labor movement had agreed to cooperate in solving the housing problem. In that connection Richard J. Gray, president of the Building Trades Department of the AFL, related that most complaints against the building trades result either from a misunderstanding of the problems or misinformation. He pointed out, for example, the technical difficulties in using spray guns in painting homes and the health hazards which these devices create for the workers; the changed construction requirements in new buildings which affect the output of bricklayers; the need for three coats of plaster, sometimes subject to criticism, under standards set by the federal government; and the cost advantages of having skilled workers rather than unskilled laborers unload and sort plumbing supplies.[12] He pledged the cooperation of his office in eliminating verified complaints of unjustified union practices.

In sharp contrast, Ralph W. Gwinn, chairman of a subcommittee of the House Committee on Education and Labor investigating restrictive, monopolistic, and racketeering practices in housing, reported at the end of 1947 that unions in the building trades use their power to enforce featherbedding, standbys, and slowdowns. He criticized lathers who quit work as soon as they have placed thirty bundles of lath or 100 square feet of gypsum board. This could often be done in six and one-half hours or less, yet they were paid for eight hours. Gwinn said that productivity was much higher on nonunion jobs. Nonunion bricklayers averaged 1,200 bricks a day while "on a similar structure, built for the same concern only 8 miles away, union bricklayers were supervised by a union steward and only 500 bricks a day were laid." [13] He felt that restrictive practices should be legally penalized.

Following the decisions of the United States Supreme Court in the early 1940's that labor unions generally are not subject to the antitrust laws, the government abandoned its attempts to use these statutes in labor cases. In an unusual action, however, the United States sued Glaziers' Local No. 27 of the Brotherhood of Painters, Decorators and Paperhangers of America in the District Court of Illinois, on March 12, 1957, for violation of the federal antitrust laws. It charged the union with restricting trade in the distribution and installation of preglazed sash and other preglazed products in the Chicago area. The government alleged that the local prevented the use of flat glass or mirrors installed in items such as windows, doors, bathroom cabinets, and shower enclosures at any place other than on the construction job site. The union denied the charges. But before the trial or adjudication, the parties agreed to a consent decree issued by the court on September 8, 1958, under which the local was enjoined from restricting the use of preglazed items, requiring reglazing of preglazed products, requiring persons to stop work on a job solely because of the use of preglazed items, and from entering into an agreement with any business organization to prohibit installation of products preglazed by workers in a union not affiliated with the painters as long as it was in the American Federation of Labor and Congress of Industrial Organizations.[14]

Labor leaders in the building trades are aware that high construction costs reduce demand and thereby cause employment to decline, but they have rarely spoken out on this matter since it is politically unwise to do so. Richard J. Gray, president of the Building Trades Department of the AFL-CIO, comprising about nineteen unions, recognized the problem. For several years he negotiated with employers. On February 5, 1958, Gray and a representative of the National Constructors Association, whose members account for ninety percent of the heavy industrial building done in the United States, announced agreement on an antifeatherbedding code. Among its ten points it provides for the end of many undesirable practices, including restrictions on the use of tools, limitations on output, union designation of foremen, starting work late and stopping early, slowdowns, and standby crews.[15] The object of this program is to cut costs and increase the demand for labor. It is evident that both sides clearly recognize the existence of much wasted labor power in the industry. The code, however, is merely advisory and can only be effective when incorporated into collective agreements. Even acceptance of the code at the international union level will not be sufficient to bring substantial improvement into the situation, because effective control over working conditions in the building trades is normally in the hands of locals. At local levels, implementation of the principles set forth has been slow and difficult because of the opposition of many unionized building workers.

Restrictive union practices in the construction industry have continued to arouse concern, however. Much public attention was focused on work stoppages at missile bases in 1961 as a result of hearings conducted by a subcommittee of the United States Senate Committee on Government Operations. One of the findings and conclusions of the subcommittee was: "Featherbedding and loafing have also been practiced at these bases."[16] The most notorious case involved the refusal of union pipefitters at Vandenberg Air Force Base in California to install prefabricated manifolds. Claiming the right to perform assembly work on the site, pipefitters sat around doing nothing for the time necessary to take apart and reassemble the manifolds.

Strikes erupted at the bases unless contractors paid craft workers for work they did not do on prefabricated parts. Such payments were often made, at the expense of taxpayers, under pressure from the armed forces which wanted the product without delay.[17] In May, 1961, special governmental machinery was set up at each missile and space site to help solve labor problems and adjust labor disputes.

Recent studies show that the working rules of unions in the construction industry restrict both technological advance and output of members. Rules include limitations on output, regulations on the use of tools, requirements for "unnecessary" men and work, prohibitions against performing certain operations in the shops rather than on the job, and protection of the jurisdiction of each craft. But restrictions generally are confined to certain building crafts involving about twenty percent of the total on-site labor—particularly in painting, plumbing, sheet metal work, electrical work, and glazing. It has been estimated that the relatively liberal working rules which prevailed during the period of high level employment following World War II raised labor costs between five and eighteen percent and that restrictions on new techniques added between three and six percent more. Union policies therefore increased on-site construction costs by a sum ranging from eight to twenty-four percent. Since labor costs normally represent about thirty percent of the selling price of a house, elimination of unreasonable union restrictions could reduce the cost to the purchaser by about five percent.[18] Other estimates support the conclusion that the cost of building homes may be increased as much as twenty or twenty-five percent through restrictive work rules.[19] It is important to stress that some featherbedding practices, such as the creation of useless jobs, are encouraged by employers who wish to hold on to skilled workers during slack seasons.[20]

During the past few years, rising labor costs, particularly in the unionized sector of the construction industry, have increased building prices to levels which have adversely affected demand for homes and commercial structures. As a result, unionized contractors have lost business to nonunion firms. Industrial establishments have increased the volume of construction work done by their own maintenance workers and by members of the industrial unions with which they bargain in order to reduce costs. These practices have been at the root of the serious controversy between the building craft unions and industrial unions, a controversy which nearly caused the disruption of the AFL-CIO on several occasions during the past decade.

Responsibility for many of the difficulties of the construction industry are widely diffused. Some of the operational and business techniques used in the industry are obsolete. Culpability for this situation must be apportioned among management, unions, and local government. Nevertheless featherbedding practices are not uniformly distributed across the country. A survey in 1959 made by *Engineering News-Record* of the McGraw-Hill chain of publications revealed that in nearly half the cities investigated construction contractors felt that featherbedding never had been and was not then serious enough to be an issue.[21]

The organization of the labor market on a craft basis has been one of the most significant factors leading to featherbedding. If industrial unionism prevailed in the industry, it is likely that there would be less resistance to the performance of work in the shop rather than on the job,[22] fewer cases of excess labor resulting from jurisdictional claims, and reduced opposition to machines and equipment affecting only small groups of union members. However, all efforts to merge the workers of the building trades into one union have failed.

The major effort to unify unionism in the building trades was made by the CIO. On July 31, 1939, it set up a Construction Workers Organizing Committee (CWOC) to negotiate with employers in the building trades. The CWOC claimed a number of advantages over rival organizations in the AFL, including a single union to bargain for all workers, elimination of jurisdictional disputes, reasonable hourly rates, and elimination of regulations against the use of new materials and new methods of production. Indeed, the CWOC cooperated in building some prefabricated housing projects. In the middle of 1940, the CWOC claimed 150 locals in thirty states concentrated in work involving factory maintenance and repair, residential construction in those areas where the CIO was strong, and road building by largely unskilled labor.

One revealing illustration of the difference in work performance between the CWOC and AFL craft unions occurred in Indiana. The CIO affiliate did not attempt to guard and preserve craft practices. It permitted use of spray painting, power equipment, wood parts precut in the mill, and facilities of a cement-mixing plant erected nearby. These methods resulted in a savings of fourteen percent over similar houses constructed by conventional methods.[23]

It is strange that Sidney Hillman, a founder of the CIO, was responsible in part for the disintegration of the CWOC. As the labor member of the National Defense Advisory Commission, he negotiated an agreement with the Building and Construction Trades Department of the AFL in July, 1941 for uniform wage rates on national defense contracts. Such governmental recognition of the dominance of AFL unions in construction work sharply reduced the ability of the CIO to make organizing advances among building workers. The CWOC became part of District 50 of the United Mine Workers in June, 1942 and for practical purposes ceased to exist.[24]

ENTERTAINMENT

Many unions active in the entertainment industry have supported featherbedding practices. These include those building trades unions whose members are engaged in construction work in theaters and motion picture studios. These unions, as has been shown, manifest a disposition to make work. Two other unions are involved—the stagehands and the musicians—though the policies followed by each of these organizations have varied. The stagehands' union, which has long waiting lists for admission, curbs membership severely in order to limit the number of workers available for jobs. The musicians' union imposes virtually no restrictions on applicants, and thereby increases competition for employment among its members. The featherbedding rules of the stagehands are burdensome on theatrical employers. One of the more glaring illustrations of this is the union requirement that a minimum of four stagehands must be used in one-man shows even if there is enough work for only one hand. Stagehands often have to be paid when cast pictures are taken for publicity purposes, even if they perform no services on the stage.[25] Billy Graham was forced to hire two stagehands, whose only duty was to carry a pitcher of water to the rostrum, when he preached at Madison Square Garden in New York City.[26]

Exorbitant costs are incurred by employers because of the strict application of jurisdictional claims by different unions. Platforms are built by carpenters, but the covering is put on by stagehands. Tables are moved by stagehands, but the lamps on them must be handled by electricians. A hat which is worn is considered part of the costume, but one which is not worn is a prop. It has also been established that costly gratuities ranging from five to fifty dollars per man must be added to wages paid in some shows to get efficient performances from the technicians.[27] Loose economic practices in the entertainment industry arise in part because producers do not ordinarily use their own money to put on a show. In the production of opera, particularly, deficits are expected almost as a rule.

The musicians' union has utilized two featherbedding devices in particular—quota or minimum-crew rules and the standby. In 1903, the American Federation of Musicians (AFM) added a provision to its bylaws permitting locals to specify the minimum number of men required to perform in theater orchestras. John R. Commons indicated, three years later, that although the idea of making work appealed to the locals and the members, there was a strong desire on the part of musicians to produce artistic music. This justified policies which specify a minimum number of men and limits each member to a single instrument at any particular engagement. Commons concluded that the musicians' "arguments are right in esthetics, and may be right in economics." He reasoned that "if the ear of the American public were cultivated to good music, it would demand more of it."[28]

Locals strong enough to do so undertook the practice of
fixing the minimum size of orchestras, but strikes and lockouts followed in the wake of such action and failure of
these efforts was typical. In 1911, the president of the musicians' union asked the delegates gathered at the annual convention to repeal the bylaw. He said: " . . . it is not accepted or recognized as a trades union principle that, in
addition to union wages and other fair conditions . . . it is
also the right of a union to stipulate how many men an
employer should employ. The employer generally objects
. . . and in this objection he has not only the public at
large, but also the sentiments of a large portion of organized
labor itself with him . . . . the President of the American
Federation of Labor . . . personally informed me that the
position of our Federation in this question is untenable." [29]
The bylaw was not repealed, however. Instead, minimum-
size crews, including those of radio staff musicians, were
subsequently authorized for other kinds of musical engage-
ments. Some state courts have enjoined union efforts to
specify the minimum number of musicians, but generally
they have permitted such activities.[30] Live musicians employed in the theaters had a limited amount of competition
from mechanical piano players beginning in the 1890's, as
well as from automatic phonographs, which appeared during the first decade of the twentieth century.

The standby policy of the AFM and its locals was intended to compel an employer to pay union members to
stand by. Each local union claimed for its own members
the work assigned to nonunion musicians, amateurs, and
traveling bands, or that performed by mechanical repro-
ducers of music. Since no services were rendered by those
standing by, the process often deteriorated to the point that
standby musicians did not even make an appearance. The
employer often paid the union a sum equal to the salaries
standbys would have earned. Although the standby is no
longer used by the national union mainly because of federal law, it is still practiced by locals in specific situations.
In New York City, for example, plays which use musical

phonograph records that are an integral part of the performance must employ four musicians, even if there is no work for them. The performer Victor Borge has used standby instrumentalists as audience stooges in his one-man show.[31]

The introduction and popularization of the commercial phonograph record during the early decades of the twentieth century served to increase public understanding and appreciation of music and led to an expansion of employment opportunities for musicians. But the development of sound motion pictures reversed the trend. In the four years beginning in 1928, 18,000 of the 22,000 musicians employed in the motion picture houses to accompany the silent films lost their jobs. Only about 200 musicians were hired to produce sound films. Thereafter, the introduction of juke boxes and wired music in restaurants and hotels and the use of recordings by radio stations displaced many other musicians. Even more so than previously, the number of regularly employed full-time musicians in the United States in the 1930's constituted a very small part of the total union membership. In 1947, about 32,400 of the 216,000 members of the AFM worked exclusively as musicians. About twice that number earned part of their living in other vocations. More than 86,000 musicians no longer played an instrument professionally because they could not find work or because they had developed other interests.[32]

Efforts by the American Federation of Musicians to protect its members against the adverse employment effects of the advance of technology—such as juke boxes, frequency modulation (FM), recordings, and television—have not been without justification. There is no doubt, however, that the methods used by the union have been crude and high-handed.

In 1937, the AFM, seeking to alleviate the problem of displacement, secured agreement from radio broadcasting stations to spend $3,000,000 for live musicians.[33] But this partial solution became inoperative in 1939 when the Antitrust Division of the Department of Justice warned employers of prosecution for restraint of trade if they continued the

practice. Further grappling with the problem of technological unemployment by the union afforded no satisfactory
means of easing the difficulties.

The union, however, felt that the technological problems
of musicians differed substantially from those typical among
other groups of employees. Musicians were displaced by
records, transcriptions, and tapes—devices which were produced by other musicians. This matter, though troublesome
to the union, at the same time has provided the leverage
necessary for negotiation of some solutions.

Early in the 1940's, under the leadership of James C.
Petrillo, the newly elected president, the AFM decided to
fight technology vigorously. Effective August 1, 1942, the
union prohibited its members from making records or other
devices for mechanical reproduction of music. No demands
were made upon employers. Instead, there was a complete
abandonment of the employment relationship. The controversy aroused widespread attention. As a result of a hearing
in February, 1943 before a subcommittee of the United
States Senate, the union modified its position and agreed
to resume work if a fund would be set up by employers
for the alleviation of unemployment. Payments were to be
based on the number of records made. The recording companies sought the help of the government. Although the
union contended that no employer-employee relationship
existed when its members ceased recording, the National
War Labor Board assumed jurisdiction on the grounds that
a strike was in progress. The union argued that pressure
by the NWLB to reestablish an employment relationship
with the recording and transcription companies was forcing its members into involuntary servitude, but it decided
to lift the ban on recordings at the end of September, 1943
when some employers agreed to set up an employment
fund administered by the union into which a specified sum
would be paid for each record made.

The conclusions reached by a majority of the panel set
up by the NWLB to study the issues were that sound films
undoubtedly had led to a decline in the number of musi-

cians employed, but that the effects of records, transcriptions, and radio were still unclear.[34] Some decrease in employment was found to have resulted from the use of juke boxes and wired music, but no figures to determine the precise extent were available.

The recording and transcription fund was intended to foster musical culture by employing live musicians to participate in free concerts, dances, and other musical performances. It was under control of the union, and its assets were derived from fees paid by recording companies. These fees were based on the selling price of records, and in the case of transcription companies, they were based on gross revenues received from transcriptions. Some firms in the industry felt that they should not contribute to a fund used for the benefit of musicians they had never employed. But they were overruled. More than $4,500,000 were collected by the fund between 1943 and 1947. Most of it was expended between 1947 and 1950 on 450,000 single-engagement jobs.

Enactment of the Labor Management Relations Act (the Taft-Hartley Act) in 1947 brought union welfare funds under federal regulation. Although the law states that a fund must be used exclusively for the benefit of employees of those employers making the contribution, the United States Supreme Court decided that relevant economic and statutory considerations could be given weight and that technical and traditional concepts were not the sole guide to be used in defining employee.[35] Nevertheless, fearing loss of control over the fund when the contracts expired at the end of 1947, the union reimposed the record ban on January 1, 1948. It emphasized that the policy was irrevocable because of increased technological unemployment brought about by the use of records, as well as the greater abundance of juke boxes, disc jockeys, and wired music. However, the establishment of a music performance trust fund under provisions satisfactory to the AFM again terminated the ban in December, 1948. Payments were made by the companies on a basis similar to that prevailing under the old arrangements—royalties based on the selling price of records and transcriptions—for the purpose of providing employment at local union scales for instrumental musicians, whether or not members of the union, and educating the general public to appreciate live instrumental music. No admission fees could be charged at concerts. The trustee of the fund, originally selected by the companies but in the future to be chosen by the Secretary of Labor, operates the fund through a series of allocations made to the locals of the union. These allocations are made mainly on a geographical basis.

In 1954 a new contract provided for higher royalty rates. In addition the record companies agreed to increase the minimum wage scale of recording musicians by ten percent for the first two years of the contract and by twenty-one percent during the last three years. This money, however, would be paid into the fund, rather than to the men. Shortly thereafter, rising dissatisfaction among recording artists, who constitute only about three percent of the union membership, became evident.

A Congressional investigation of the fund took place in 1956. At that time, about 51,000 of the 250,000 members of the union were engaged primarily as professional musicians, of whom fewer than 10,000 did any work in the fields of phonograph records, motion pictures, filmed television, or broadcast radio and television music.[36] Complaints were voiced by some members, led by those in the Los Angeles local, that wages of musicians in the recording industry were not rising because employers were making increased payments to the trust fund. Objections to the undue burden carried by Los Angeles and New York musicians in supporting the music performance trust funds were expressed, and objection was made to the use of resources of the funds for the benefit of other than those who are unemployed professional musicians. No significant changes in the operation of the fund occurred as a result of the hearings, but a small rival union of musicians was established in Los Angeles.

A series of suits instituted in the California courts by some of the recording musicians to recover the twenty-one percent wage increase which had been diverted to the fund was long and costly. But these musicians were successful, and in 1960 the AFM reached a monetary settlement with them.[37] As a result of some successful organizational activity and contractual arrangements achieved by the dual union, as well as the court litigation, the AFM discontinued the twenty-one percent wage scale payments into the fund when the contract expired at the end of 1958. Instead, it negotiated wage and pension benefits for the recording musicians. In 1961, the rival union was dissolved when the AFM agreed that fifty percent of the royalties received on all new records produced would be paid to recording musicians.

Although a large part of the programming of radio stations is made up of music, much of the music is recorded. The AFM has devoted considerable effort to increase the number of musicians employed by radio stations, but its economic strength generally has been exercised effectively only against the networks and their affiliated outlets. A small fraction of radio stations use staff musicians; some employ a limited number of musicians with regularity; a few hire them on a single engagement basis only. But most of the stations depend entirely on recorded music. Techniques used by the union to increase radio employment have included a requirement that standbys be employed whenever amateurs, nonunion instrumentalists, or traveling musicians from other jurisdictions participated on programs. This tactic was brought to an end by the passage of the Lea Act in 1946. Another measure to increase employment, first used in 1945, was the rule that double crews of musicians would have to be employed on programs duplicated over AM and FM. Neither network nor independent AM stations could feed musical programs to FM stations. This decision was not rescinded until 1948, when the union concluded that potential employment opportunities for musicians on frequency modulation stations were limited in the foreseeable future and the Lea Act might be applicable to restrictive actions.

But AFM policy toward the emerging television broadcasting industry which began commercial service in 1941, was quite different. Between 1945 and 1948, the union prohibited its members from performing on any television program. Fear of unemployment was at the root of the policy. The ultimate prevalence of kinescope or canned television was the specter. Since television seemed destined to become a leading form of entertainment, the AFM wanted to make a carefully considered decision. In 1946, in a contract with the film producers, the use of motion picture musical sound track on television was prohibited. But in 1950 and 1951 the union reversed itself. Agreements with motion picture companies permitted films to be televised, provided that five percent of the leasing receipts would be paid into a music performance trust fund. Arrangements were also made regarding television film jingles and spot announcements. In 1954 a television film contract was signed with the networks permitting kinescopes to be made and shown more than once, provided payments were made into the trust fund. No payment was necessary for the first showing on an affiliated network station in any city. Royalties received by the phonograph record and television film funds are commingled and administered jointly.

Union pressures upon the radio broadcasting industry to increase staff employment, to keep amateurs and nonmembers from playing unless the station agreed to pay standbys, and to reduce the use of musical records attracted much public attention and caused considerable resentment. In 1946 these activities culminated in the Lea Act. The report of the Congressional committee in the House of Representatives which recommended enactment of the law declared that the legislation was intended to protect the broadcasting industry against exactions imposed by the musicians' union, exactions which had already reached millions of dollars.[38]

PRINTING

Like construction and entertainment, printing is dominated by craft unions. For a long time, a specific makework tactic practiced by the typographers dominated featherbedding discussions concerning the industry. More recently, new forms of technology have appeared which are intensifying labor problems and involving most of the other unions in the industry.

Featherbedding among printers, which consists primarily of resetting type which has already been set, is an old and established custom. When the National Labor Relations Board found in 1949 that this useless reproduction work does not violate the Taft-Hartley Act, it stated that the practice occupies about five percent of the time workers spend on the job. But the NLRB said that payment for nonproduction time when it is incident to the employment itself, such as paid rest or vacation periods, is in no way considered an exaction. Remunerating typographical reproduction work represents an integral part of the wage structure of printing employees and is similar to the guaranteed annual wage, generally recognized as legal, which frequently involves payment for nonproductive time.[39]

Reproduction, known as bogus or deadhorse, is the practice under which local newspaper advertisements are copied after they have already been printed in the newspaper. The general laws of the International Typographical Union provide that when there is an interchange or purchase of matter in the form of plates or matrices between newspapers or between newspapers and job offices, the plates or matrices must be reset and corrected as nearly like the original as possible. Materials other than local advertisements, including national advertisements, are normally exempt from the provisions in contracts negotiated by the local unions.

Advertisers ordinarily submit advertisements to a newspaper in the form of a matrix prepared by a local specialty printing shop or in the composing room of another newspaper. Since newspapers charge primarily for space rather

than labor, the cost to the advertiser is the same as if the
original copy had been submitted. After a plate is made
from the matrix and the ad is run off, a tear sheet is placed
on the bogus hook for reproduction. Later the advertisement
is reproduced and corrected; it is then immediately con-
signed to the "hell box" and melted down. Normally bogus
is performed during those periods of the day, week, or season
when the volume of work is low. It rarely involves overtime,
but occasionally it necessitates hiring extra compositors.
These extra employees would not necessarily be assigned
to do the bogus.

The problem related to bogus type arose in 1871 when
one of the daily newspapers in New Albany, Indiana, began
to borrow type set in a Louisville, Kentucky, daily newspaper composing room. At that time most typesetters were
paid on a piecework basis, and earnings and employment
were related to the volume of typesetting done by the
newspaper. Despite the fact that no type was set, the local
union in New Albany required the employer to pay its
printers the wages they would have earned if they had done
the work. The local wanted to protect the jobs of its
members and reduce unfair competitive advantages of newspapers which did not have the work performed. The employers appealed to the national officers of the union, but
the ITU convention decided in 1872 that the transfer of
matter from one firm to another should not be allowed.[40]

Subsequently and gradually such restrictions were incorporated in the general laws of the ITU. But because of the
many new problems arising by the turn of the century, such
as the introduction of the linotype machines, plates, photoen-
gravings, and matrices, the severity and vigor of nonunion
competition, and the special situations confronting printers
in different parts of the country, reproduction was introduced to protect the working opportunities of union members. The national union officially recognized the policy of
reproduction in 1901, although local union contracts had
already incorporated such clauses earlier. For example, the

Chicago local has had such a provision in its agreements since 1897.

At first, local advertisements were set almost exclusively in composing rooms of newspapers and advertisers tended to submit copy to those newspapers with the best type and facilities. Reproduction clauses, encouraged by some newspapers, served to eliminate the unfair competitive advantage of those obtaining matrices without cost. More recently, advertisements generally have been set in commercial shops, and the transfer of matrices between newspapers has declined. National advertisements, on the other hand, were always supplied by advertising agencies and this may explain why the union did not adopt reproduction rules in this sector of the business.[41]

By 1940 the national union had evolved a series of detailed regulations in its general laws governing reproduction work. These regulations were a standard part of agreements negotiated by locals. Locals were permitted to work out their own arrangements regarding time limits for setting bogus, exemptions for matrices received from commercial compositors or for national ads, interchanges between English and foreign language publications, and generally any matter other than local advertisements.[42]

The bogus dispute centers around the claim by publishers that the practice is costly, wasteful, and useless, that it creates unnecessary work, and that occasionally it requires extra workers. Thus in the late 1940's, the cost of setting bogus was about $150,000 a year at *The New York Times*, $50,000 a year at the *Chicago Herald-American*, and $5,000 annually at the *Rochester Democrat and Chronicle*.[43] On December 1, 1960, there were 51,216 printers earning $6,229,379.45 per week employed by newspapers.[44] Assuming reproduction time and its equivalent to be only three percent, the annual cost of bogus to the industry is about $10,000,000.[45] The union position stresses that reproduction eliminates unfair competition among newspaper publishers who otherwise would secure matrices free of charge, stabilizes employment by creating work during periods when there is a lull in activity, maintains a labor force of adequate size, and prevents employers from eliminating printers by establishing joint composing rooms to set advertisements.

A provision in the Taft-Hartley Act raised a question concerning the legality of bogus. But the NLRB, the Circuit Court of Appeals, and the United States Supreme Court all found that no restrictions on the practice were imposed by the legislation because printers were performing a service, even if it is not needed. There were, however, important discrepancies concerning the matter of reproduction among the general laws of the international, the provisions in the local contracts, and the actual practices in the industry. These discrepancies were apparent to union officials. As a result of the decision of the 1959 convention, the following year the executive council of the ITU sent a questionnaire to the 782 locals of the union inquiring about reproduction practices. Of the 558 locals which responded, 361 stated that they were not doing reproduction work, 110 said they were setting bogus, and eighty-six declared that although the local advertisements were being placed on the bogus hook, no reproduction work was performed during the month the questionnaire was received. Furthermore, international union officers were skeptical about the 110 locals which claimed they did bogus. A supplementary check of fifty-nine locals located throughout the United States and Canada made at the same time by a special representative of the ITU disclosed that only about two to five percent of the locals he visited were doing bogus.[46] Elsewhere it was generally traded by the local for time off, overtime, coffee breaks, sick leave, and maintenance of a stable crew. Often only token performance of bogus occurred. It was also reported that some locals were enforcing reproduction on one paper but not on another in the same area.

These two surveys convinced Elmer Brown, president of the ITU, that the reproduction regulations of the international union should be modified. At the 1960 convention he suggested that the clause in the constitution dealing with this matter be amended and shifted to the bylaws to give locals the option of exchanging reproduction provisions for some other benefit, such as a national pension plan. Some of the delegates were extremely hostile to Brown's proposal; a majority of those who spoke on the issue opposed any changes. It was clear from their remarks that bogus represented to them a cushion against unemployment. The convention decided to submit the issue to the entire membership. When the union balloted on the question in a referendum held in October, two months after the convention, the proposal to effect a change in the rules and grant locals the option of negotiating a national old-age pension and welfare plan as an alternative, although vigorously supported by the officers, was defeated by a vote of 41,909 to 30,863.[47]

The reproduction policy of the union remains in effect, but its practice by individual locals is being discontinued or unofficially replaced by diverse concessions from employers. Though this aspect of featherbedding in the printing industry has been given the greatest public attention historically, the prolonged newspaper strike in New York City that began in December, 1962 and continued for 114 days, through the end of March, 1963, revealed another and probably more serious makework problem at the center of the controversy. The specter of unemployment which reproduction was intended to suppress seems relatively minor when compared to the potential impact of the teletypesetters on the working opportunities of printers.

Rising costs of production in the newspaper industry has encouraged experimentation with electronic and photographic processes in efforts to eliminate typesetting, stereotyping, and engraving.[48] A major advance was made with the introduction of the teletypesetter which was demonstrated in 1928 and first used in 1931. This mechanical innovation sets into type copy which has been transcribed by the operator into code-perforated tape; the perforations provide controls for operating the keyboard of a line casting machine to select matrices for composing slugs and for other operations required to simulate manual performance. Output is increased between 50 and 100 percent over manual operation.[49] Furthermore, teletypesetter tape produced at one point may be transmitted over wires for any distance and copied at any other number of places. The adoption of this invention was slow, but by 1956 it was used by the major wire services to supply news to almost 800 daily newspapers.[50]

Teletypesetting is quite common outside of New York City, but within the city only *The New York Times* and *The Wall Street Journal* had any tape operations at the beginning of 1963. Although *The Wall Street Journal* has been using tapes for more than a decade, the agreement with the printers local requires a typesetter, who performs no service, to sit before many of the automatic machines. Many of the New York newspapers are interested in tapes only for financial listings and sports tabulations or for the texts of documents and speeches, since they have their own reporters, editorial staff, and correspondents. It has been estimated that the *New York Herald Tribune*, which uses between eighty and ninety man-hours each day to set its stock and bond tables at an annual cost of $250,000 to $300,-000, could reduce the time necessary to do so to less than a half-hour a day without employing a single compositor by using Associated Press or United Press International teletypesetter service.[51] The possibilities of labor displacement are evident.

Although small newspapers are inclined to the general use of teletypesetter facilities of news services, adoption by the *Los Angeles Times*, which has no ITU contract, of an electronic computer foreshadows even greater problems from automation. With this advance over the teletypesetter, it is estimated that at least fifty of the 100 typesetters at the *Los Angeles Times* will be eliminated in the next few years.[52] Other new machines further threaten to reduce employment opportunities.

The leadership of the printers local in New York City is resisting technological advance because it fears that the impact on jobs will be very great and that even a policy of protecting those currently employed might ultimately lead to the end of work opportunities for printers at newspapers. But it is also anxious to protect the opportunities of men who are currently part-time substitute printers. The agreement reached in the New York City strike provided that the use of teletypesetter tapes by the newspapers would be limited to financial tables of the stock exchanges provided by the press services. In return, the newspapers agreed not to layoff any printers because of this change and to establish a joint committee to determine the proportion of the resulting savings which should be shared with the members of the local.

Though the existence of featherbedding in the printing industry has usually been associated with the typesetters, other branches have not been free of complaints. Efforts by the pressmen and their assistants to maintain employment as presses became larger and more automatic generally failed under pressure by employers.[53] A report by the Illinois State Chamber of Commerce found that the union required a substantially greater number of men to operate the newspaper presses than would be adequate. Other undesirable practices prohibit switching pressmen from one machine to another, require a full day's pay for as little as two hours' work, and impose an excessive crew on new and improved stereotype machines. The study suggested that the costs of overmanned presses might exceed those stemming from bogus.[54] Manning variations for printing presses in different localities are common under union contracts.[55]

Until 1889 employees in the printing industry belonged to one union. Technological change, particularly division of the functions of the printing craft into composition and presswork, led to a series of schisms and the establishment of a number of distinct international unions in the trade. But more recently, as a result of the dimming of craft outlines that were once sharp, there has been an increasing number of jurisdictional disputes among the several trade unions in the industry. It is probable that these issues, which are likely to increase in number, will be resolved only by consolidation and merger of the separate organizations.

Several work assignment conflicts concerning technology and displacement in the printing industry have come before the National Labor Relations Board recently for resolution. In one case, for example, the Board decided that a new card camera machine purchased by a commercial printing firm should be operated by pressmen rather than compositors because area practice and contractual claims favored the former group. The factors of the skill of the employees involved and the efficient operation of the business favored neither the members of the pressmen's union nor those of the typographical union.[56] In another and more difficult case, the Board held that composing room employees (International Typographical Union) on a newspaper were entitled to perform the work on a new photocomposition process rather than photoengravers (International Photoengravers' Union) or photographers from the editorial department (American Newspaper Guild). The majority of the Board ruled that typographers should get the work because otherwise employment opportunities would decline for them. The new process had replaced the hot metal methods of composition using the services of typographers. There were four opinions handed down by the NLRB in the three-to-two decision.[57]

MISCELLANEOUS

Featherbedding has not been important in other industries or among other groups of workers, despite the fact that from time to time there are reports and complaints of makework practices in sectors of the economy other than those discussed above. Generally, however, such featherbedding does not involve union rules. For example, the report made to Congress in 1963 by the Securities and Exchange Commission on the adequacy of investor protection in the securities markets stated that the exchanges have not automated sufficiently to reduce costs. The study group found that: "The securities markets are not inherently more immune from featherbedding than any other business." [58] Much opposition to mechanization and automation stems from the older men who own and control the brokerage houses and are averse to new methods that will eliminate their functions and duties on the floors of the exchanges.

Manufacturing industry typically is free from featherbedding because unionization is more recent, industrial unions dominate the labor market, and management has been relatively careful in negotiating agreements. Problems frequently concern work rules which have become obsolete but which were never intended to provide makework. Among the mass production industries, steel provides an illustration of the issues.

The longest steel dispute in American history took place in 1959-1960. The most important issue concerned the local work rules. The companies, faced by changing technology, foreign competition, and competitive domestic products, insisted on the unlimited right to alter work rules in order to manage business more effectively and improve operations. But the union feared such authority would lead to the loss of job protection.

Beginning in 1947 the union and major steel producers specifically agreed to preserve generally established local working conditions, such as crew size, work loads, job content, seniority practices, wash-up arrangements, overtime distribution systems, relief periods and coffee breaks, spell arrangements, safety precautions, and lunch periods. These provisions were incorporated in what is known as Section 2B of the United States Steel Corporation contract. But in 1959 the industry demanded the right to change work rules if money could be saved thereby. On July 13, David J. McDonald, president of the steelworkers' union, wrote the steel companies that the union does not oppose and the contract permits technological change and automation of equipment, but that management may alter prevailing work practices unilaterally only if it introduces new technology or automation. The following day, management acknowledged the accuracy of the union's position, but it contended that it must be free to change rules concerning methods of production, reassignment of duties, and elimination of unjustifiable idle time even when there has been no heavy investment for new facilities. Industry spokesmen, however, did not place emphasis on charges of featherbedding. Richard C. Cooper of the United States Steel Corporation, chief labor negotiator for the industry, said that the difficulties are "wasteful practices that have grown up over the years—not featherbedding or make-work practices deliberately installed." [59]

Practices are protected under Section 2B only if they have been the regularly accepted way of doing things at the local plant. Should conditions which led to the introduction of a practice change, management may alter the terms of employment. Curtailment of production, for example, justifies a reduction in the size of the crew. It is the well-established and mutually agreed upon arrangements, ordinarily carefully considered by the company when put into effect, which are not subject to unilateral modification. The purpose of Section 2B is to balance the desire of the company for flexibility and growth with the need of employees for stability.

George W. Taylor, chairman of the board of inquiry appointed by President Eisenhower under the emergency provisions of the Taft-Hartley Act, summed up the testimony taken at the hearings by saying that steel " . . . companies have rather wide latitude in introducing technological change and adjusting manpower accordingly, this is a practice which, I assure you, many other industries would give a great deal to have." [60] The issue was not over technological change, but was rather one of obsolete work rules. The company wants a change in the interest of more efficient operation.

Settlement of the dispute in January, 1960 provided for the establishment of a committee to study local working conditions and another dealing with human relations research. The former became dormant soon after it was organized because of inability to select an impartial chairman. The second, which required no neutral members, undertook to study many issues.

Although both the United States Steel Company and the steelworkers' union were free to reopen their labor contract on May 1, 1963, this was not done. Instead informal talks for more than five months by the human relations committee and its subcommittees, set up as part of the 1959 strike settlement, led to an extension of the agreement to May 1, 1965, with the possibility that it may be extended again. Workers did not get any wage increase. In the face of declining employment in the steel industry resulting from technological advance, the union was concerned to spread the work among its members and concentrated its energies on increasing income and job security.

The new understanding, approved by the eleven major steel producers participating in the talks, provides for a vacation of thirteen weeks once every five years for half of each company's employees, improved welfare benefits, further limitation on the right of the companies to have work that could be done in the plant contracted out, restrictions on the type of production work supervisors may do, and discussions with the union before determining whether to use overtime or to recall laid off workers.[61] Extended vacations will be financed by company contributions into a fund. Estimates are that about 20,000 new jobs will be provided in the industry now employing 487,000 workers.

There are several ways to eliminate restrictive work rules in steel manufacturing. The best method is to develop and introduce technological changes which make the practices unnecessary. This device has been employed successfully by management.[62] Otherwise, tighter supervision must be instituted, educational campaigns conducted, bargaining procedures used, or financial arrangements made. It is not usually good strategy, however, to contend that management has the right to change rules.

Chapter VII

FEATHERBEDDING AND THE LAW

The laws of the land have not been effective in controlling featherbedding practices. Although the federal government has been more concerned with this issue than any of the states and has enacted several laws bearing on this matter, not much success has been achieved in curbing makework. The statutes dealing with work restrictions are generally weak, sometimes inconsistent, and often of doubtful enforceability. Indeed, at the state level, significant legislation protecting featherbedding practices in the railroad industry has been enacted.

There has been one federal court case dealing with featherbedding which was decided on the basis of the common law. In 1897 a circuit court held that a boycott by two unions to compel a manufacturer of casks and barrels to discontinue use of a barrel-hooping machine is an unlawful conspiracy.[1] The public at large, the court said, should not be deprived of the benefits of labor-saving machines. Generally, however, courts are not able to declare strikes against technological change illegal. The futility of such strikes and the harm they cause society are insufficient grounds for holding the union objective of preventing displacement unlawful.[2]

The role of the government in regulating featherbedding has been hesitant and inchoate. "The task of sorting out permissible union activities from those that should be prosecuted is exceedingly difficult, particularly as in the past unions have been allowed to do almost whatever they wished to promote their interests, as long as it was confined to the use of purely economic coercion. But economic pressures backed up by monopolistic control of labor can be vicious, ruthless, and irresistible." [3]

Only isolated featherbedding practices are subject to federal proscription by statute. Makework rules which restrain trade are prohibited by the antitrust laws only if the union has conspired with employers to obtain them. The Hobbs Act applies if the union imposes makework by threats of physical violence. Under the Lea Act, featherbedding and makework by musicians are illegal in the radio broadcasting industry. Finally, the Taft-Hartley Act makes it illegal for workers to be paid when services are not proffered and not rendered. Otherwise, making and spreading work is permitted under federal law. State legislation shows no pattern.

FEDERAL ANTITRUST LAWS

The Sherman Antitrust Act, as passed in 1890, did not specifically exempt labor union activity from its provisions. There was considerable controversy as to whether the law applied to unions, but in the 1890's the federal district courts and in 1908 the United States Supreme Court decided that it did. The labor movement fought vigorously to bar application of the law to union activities, and apparent legislative relief was obtained through enactment of the Clayton Act in 1914. Since the Sherman Act was enforced against labor organizations by the use of injunctions, Section 20 of the Clayton Act drastically restricted the use of injunctions against specifically enumerated union practices from which the taint of illegality was removed. Although Gompers considered the law to be a Magna Charta, the United States Supreme Court limited exemption of union conduct from antitrust violation to those activities directed against an employer by his own employees. The Court found violations when unions engaged in secondary boycotts against dealers who did not employ members of these unions or who sold goods produced by employers with whom the unions had an existing dispute over conditions of employment. [4] Further agitation criticizing judicial interpretation of

Congressional intent led to passage of the Norris-LaGuardia
Act in 1932. This law established that the allowable
area of industrial conflict and union activity was not to
be limited to immediate employer-employee situations and
further narrowed the areas in which federal courts issue
injunctions. The three Acts must be considered jointly to
determine whether labor union activity violates the antitrust laws.

The result of the new enactment was that the circumstances under which labor was subject to antitrust proceedings were sharply reduced. For a time featherbedding by
the building trades unions appeared to be in conflict with
the laws. In 1939 Thurman W. Arnold, Assistant Attorney
General in charge of the Antitrust Division of the United
States Department of Justice announced the government's
policy regarding the kind of labor union activity that would
be prosecuted under the antitrust laws. Since the Antitrust
Division at that time was primarily concerned with restraints on the distribution of goods, and did not wish to
involve itself in labor activities directly, the emphasis of its
work fell on practices carried on by the building trades
unions. These unions, the Division felt, refused to permit
new products or processes to be used if changes would
enable buildings to be erected with fewer hours of labor.
Such behavior, the Antitrust Division said, goes beyond
the legitimate role of unions to bargain collectively regarding wages, hours, health, safety, and the speed-up system.
Types of unreasonable restraint subject to prosecution included actions which prevent the use of cheaper material,
improved equipment, and more efficient methods. It also
included actions which compel hiring useless and unnecessary labor.[5] The efforts were effective. "Indefensible restrictions by labor were being abandoned as soon as
prosecutions were commenced. Unions appeared to be willing to accept decrees which bound them to discontinue
these restrictions. Though the unions made loud public
protest many influential labor leaders confidentially admitted
that such curbs were necessary."[6] This program, strongly

denounced by the labor movement, was short-lived, however, because of judgments reached by the United States Supreme Court.

The policy of the Attorney General to apply the Sherman Antitrust Act to featherbedding practices, enunciated in 1939, received a severe setback from the Supreme Court in 1941. The Court found that a secondary boycott and jurisdictional dispute to force an employer to replace one group of workers by another does not violate the antitrust laws.[7] Labor unions were virtually exempt from prosecution under these statutes. But in subsequent decisions the Court went further. It affirmed decisions of lower courts that it was not illegal for unions to prohibit the use of cheaper prefabricated and improved building materials in construction work through secondary boycotts;[8] to force an employer to hire the same number of men after he installs improved labor-saving cement mixers;[9] or to ban production of musical phonograph records in order to bring about the employment of live musicians.[10] The Supreme Court then announced that only when organized workers combine with employers to restrain trade and monopolize the marketing of goods are union actions deemed violations of the antitrust laws.[11]

Since these decisions in the early 1940's, the antitrust laws have not been considered applicable to trade union featherbedding. From time to time, however, it has been suggested that the statutes might well serve to control the practices. Sumner H. Slichter has suggested that if a neutral board set up for the purpose were to find a collective bargaining agreement providing for unreasonably wasteful use of labor or restrictive prohibitions on new technology, application of the antitrust laws would be in order.[12]

THE HOBBS ACT

The Antiracketeering Act (known also as the Hobbs Act since the amendments of 1946) is a federal statute enacted in 1934. It outlaws violence or intimidation having the purpose of exacting money from employers engaged in interstate commerce. But it includes a clause exempting from its provisions a payment of wages by an employer to an employee. Some featherbedding cases have been prosecuted under this enactment. The courts found that the law applies to union officials extorting from employers for their personal advantage even when undertaken in conjunction with demands for wage increases.[13] In 1942, however, the Supreme Court held that the law does not bar truck drivers and their union from requiring and compelling owners of each interstate truck entering New York City to employ or, as an alternative, to pay a day's wages to a local union driver or helper. The Court declared that the law may not be applied even if violence is threatened or used by a union unless it is shown that money is obtained without the union or its members rendering or being willing to render adequate services.[14] Militant labor activity, the Court said, was not subject to this law. But the violence disclosed by the record could be prosecuted under ordinary criminal law.

This decision led Congress to amend the law in 1946 to prohibit robbery and extortion or any attempt or conspiracy to commit acts which interfere with interstate commerce. It seems clear that in amending the Antiracketeering Act, Congress was primarily concerned with the improper means used by unions, specifically violence, rather than the improper objective of featherbedding. Indeed, the House committee which proposed the Hobbs bill rejected two alternative measures dealing with featherbedding.

Although the number of cases prosecuted in the past decade have been few, the new provisions have proved to be more effective. When a local of laborers in the hod carriers' union attempted to exact money from employers for makework services, the highest court decided, in 1956, that the law makes it a criminal offense for a union to threaten to use force or to use it in order to make an employer pay wages for imposed, unwanted, superfluous, and fictitious services.[15] It held that the commission of extortion does not depend on whether the union agent receives direct personal benefits. In another case, a circuit court held that extortion induced by threat of economic harm constitutes a violation of the law even if there is no fear of force or violence.[16] The defendants were convicted for extorting money from the trucking companies under threat of continuing a strike.

THE LEA ACT

The arbitrary tactics used by James C. Petrillo, president of the musicians' union, in collective bargaining negotiations with the broadcasting industry evoked considerable fury and antagonism. When the union barred its members in 1942 from making phonograph records and required radio stations to pay standby time, the government brought suit under the antitrust laws to enjoin these practices. A federal district court found that the Norris-LaGuardia Act prevented the issuance of an injunction because the demands related to conditions of employment.[17] Congressional and public criticism of this decision and resentment against the policy of the union prohibiting the broadcast of noncommercial educational concerts led to passage of the Lea Act, or Anti-Petrillo Act, in 1946, as an amendment to the Communications Act of 1934.

The Lea Act makes it a criminal offense to use force or threats to compel a radio station: to hire more employees than the number needed to perform actual services; to pay for services which are not to be performed or men who have not been employed; to pay more than once for services rendered; to refrain from broadcasting noncommercial educational or cultural programs; and to refrain from broadcasting foreign radio programs. The Act was held unconstitutional by a federal district court in a case in which Petrillo was accused of attempting to compel a radio station in Chicago, which used musical records and transcriptions during ninety percent of its broadcast time, to employ six musicians when the station felt it needed only three. In 1947, on appeal, the United States Supreme Court upheld the con-

stitutionality of the law in a five-to-three decision.[18] Petrillo
was subsequently acquitted, however, because it could not
be established that he knew or was told the radio station
did not need three additional musicians or that he intended
that the men in dispute would not perform actual work.[19]
The court noted, however, that the three union musicians
whose services were withdrawn did not return to work and
were not replaced. Instead, their services as record librarians
were assumed by other employees of the station.

No further test cases have been brought to the courts
under this Act but featherbedding abuses have not been
an issue of significance in the broadcasting industry since
1946. Several interesting cases, however, have been proc-
essed in the state courts. In 1954, a New York court considered a demand by the musicians' union that a broad-
caster replace recordings with live musicians. The judge
enjoined picketing because he found that there was no
lawful labor objective in this instance under common law;
he added that picketing also violated the Lea Act.[20] Judgment in the case was based in part on an earlier New York
ruling in which the highest state court had declared that
"for a union to insist that machinery be discarded in order
that manual labor may take its place and thus secure additional opportunity of employment is not a lawful labor objective."[21] In Michigan, the state Supreme Court found that
antiinjunction acts do not apply in all featherbedding cases,
and it enjoined two unions from forcing a theater owner
to hire six musicians whom he said he did not need.[22]

THE TAFT-HARTLEY ACT

The Taft-Hartley Act, or Labor Management Relations
Act, includes a provision which deals with featherbedding.
It is an unfair labor practice, but not a crime, under Section
8(b)(6), for a union or its agents to cause an employer to
pay for services which are not performed or not to be
performed. Although at one point during consideration of
the bill provisions more like those in the Lea Act were

included, it was decided to limit the scope of the restrictions in order to identify fairly clear cases of behavior considered illegal.

The original bill passed by the House of Representatives made it illegal for a union to attempt to compel an employer to accede to featherbedding practices. Featherbedding was specifically defined in the bill to include employment of unnecessary workers, all of whom perform actual services, and payment by an employer to persons who perform no work at all. The Senate and House conferees eliminated the first category but accepted the second. The final version of the bill, however, did not use the term "featherbedding." Thus, while the House had proscribed practices similar to those barred by the Lea Act—including employing an unreasonable number of persons, paying money in lieu of employing persons, paying for services more than once, paying for services not rendered, and paying a tax for the use of machinery or imposing a restriction on its use—the provisions were not acceptable to Senator Robert A. Taft, chief draftsman of the law. Taft felt it was not practical to give a board or court the power to determine the number of men necessary to perform a job.[23] He sought to avoid the controversial features of the Lea Act.

Violation of Section 8(b)(6) of the law subjects the offender to a cease and desist order of the NLRB or, if the Board finds it necessary to do so, the Board may secure a temporary injunction. The violator may also be required to repay the amount which has been exacted.

Clarification of the effect of the LMRA on featherbedding was provided by two United States Supreme Court decisions in 1953, made necessary by a conflict in interpretation of Section 8(b)(6) between the Sixth and Seventh Circuit Courts of Appeals. The Supreme Court virtually eliminated any possible effectiveness of the featherbedding provision. It found that the law does not apply in cases where payment is made for work not needed or not wanted as long as workers are ready to do the job. Only where the union demands payment for work which it has no intention of hav-

ing done or which cannot be done does a violation of the
law occur.

One case involved printing. The American Newspaper
Publishers Association, whose membership owns newspapers
which have more than ninety percent of circulation of daily
and Sunday papers in the United States, brought charges
before the National Labor Relations Board against the
International Typographical Union and its officers for violat-
ing the antifeatherbedding provision of the Taft-Hartley
Act. It contended that insistence by the ITU that printers
should be paid for setting bogus type is an unfair labor
practice. The NLRB dismissed the charges. The Seventh
Circuit Court of Appeals upheld the Board. The Supreme
Court, in affirming the decision of the Seventh Circuit, stated
that bogus typesetting is not a violation of the law.[24]

The other case concerned musicians. The Akron Local of
the American Federation of Musicians, following the prevalent practice of the union, required employers using
traveling name bands to employ local musicians to play
before and after the performance and during intermissions.
A theater chain refused to employ local musicians for performances or on a standby basis, and the local union barred
traveling musicians from playing at the theater. Featherbedding charges by the employer were dismissed by the
National Labor Relations Board. It found the union was
seeking employment for musicians ready to perform services.
The Circuit Court, however, held that the local violated
the Taft-Hartley Act by attempting to force a theater to
hire musicians it did not want. In reversing the Sixth Circuit, the Supreme Court found that a demand by musicians
to play in connection with certain theater programs when
management feels their work is unnecessary does not conflict with Section 8(b)(6).[25] The Court concluded that
Congress had decided to limit featherbedding practices only
slightly by the Taft-Hartley law. Section 8(b)(6) does not
prohibit bona fide makework or payment for vacation, lunch
periods, rest, or waiting periods.

Three justices dissented from each decision. Chief Justice Fred M. Vinson and Justice Tom C. Clark felt that both cases involved violations of the law. Strangely, Justice William O. Douglas thought the newspaper case represented featherbedding while the musicians case did not. Justice Robert H. Jackson came to the opposite conclusion in each instance. Douglas considered bogus not only unwanted by employers but also useless to them, whereas the music performed would not necessarily be useless to the patrons. Jackson decided that the work in both situations is unwanted by employers, but that bogus is based on an old custom established by mutual consent to which the other terms of employment have been adjusted. He felt that the musicians, on the other hand, merely substituted a new device for the illegal standby arrangement in order to achieve the same result which Congressional action had condemned.

Court decisions emasculated the potential usefulness of Section 8(b)(6) in reducing the number of featherbedding practices. Although there were about 130 charges filed with the NLRB under this provision between 1954 and 1963, only one case, and that in 1954, dealing with this question was actually decided by the Board subsequent to the rulings by the United States Supreme Court. The charge, involving the electrical workers, was dismissed.[26] However, there have been a variety of administrative decisions by the general counsel of the NLRB interpreting Section 8(b)(6).

A decision by the United States Supreme Court in 1961 forced the NLRB to take a hand in determining questions of technological displacement connected with jurisdictional disputes. The Wagner Act did not deal directly with jurisdictional disputes over work assignments, but Sections 8(b)(4)(D) and 10(k) of the Taft-Hartley Act prohibited picketing and threats of picketing in support of claims by a union that its members should perform work done by others. These sections authorized the Board to determine the dispute if the parties were not able to settle voluntarily. Until 1961 it was the Board's policy to ascertain whether a union

claiming work had a contract or Board certification giving
it rights to those functions. If not, the NLRB held that
assignment made by the employer was controlling. The
Supreme Court reversed this policy in the Columbia Broadcasting System case and required the Board to make an
affirmative award of work in dispute to one of the claimants
on the merits.[27] In effect, compulsory arbitration of interunion disputes prevails.

Recent technological change has diluted the craft duties
of many workers and eliminated the jobs of others. In some
instances, employees with little skill are replaced by machines requiring highly skilled technicians. Very often craft
unions are involved in the disputes which arise. The Board
decides these cases on an individual basis, but there have
been a number of relevant factors which are considered.
These include previous certifications, existence of collective
bargaining contracts, rulings by the AFL-CIO or its subsidiary bodies, awards of arbitrators, past practices of the
employer, custom and practice in the industry and area,
skill and training required for the job, similarities to other
work in cases of new jobs or processes, efficiency of operations, and economy and safety. Each case, the Board said,
would be judged on the basis of common sense and experience rather than precedent. But disputed work is
awarded to a group of employees rather than to a union
itself in order to avoid requiring employers to hire members of a particular union in violation of Sections 8(a)(2)
and 8(a)(3) of the Taft-Hartley Act.

Using the enumerated principles, the NLRB has awarded
the job of operating electric overhead cranes in a machine
shop to electricians rather than machinists.[28] The work of
adjusting and maintaining automatic machines for cigarette
packaging when hand packing of cartons is eliminated was
awarded to tobacco production workers, not machinists.[29]
The Board assigned hod carriers rather than operating
engineers to the work of starting, maintaining, and stopping
plaster mixers and plaster applicators.[30] Machines which replaced planers and cut out seventy-five percent of the pre-

vious working time of machinists and patternmakers was assigned to machinists.[31] Clearly, determination of jurisdictional disputes connected with technological change is becoming an important Board function.

Section 302 of the LMRA, broadened by amendments in 1959, also bears on featherbedding. It is unlawful for an employer to make payments to representatives of his employees or for representatives to demand or accept such payments. This portion of the law was originally designed to deal primarily with problems relating to the checkoff and employee pension and welfare funds. A provision was added to this section in 1959 making it illegal for a union or its representative to demand a fee from a truck driver or his employer to unload cargo, except as compensation for services performed. If violence or intimidation is involved in taking a fee, the Antiracketeering Act also applies.

Other provisions of the Taft-Hartley Act, not specifically designed to deal with featherbedding, have been used with some success to combat union practices restricting output. For example, unfair labor practices have been found: when employees were induced not to handle prefabricated material in order to force less efficient processing on the job site;[32] when an employee was discharged who refused to slow down his work to a rate of speed set by the union;[33] and when an employer was forced to hire union members less competent than the best workers available in the market because of union pressure.[34] These activities have been considered violations of Sections 8(a)(1), 8(a)(3), 8(b)(1) (A), 8(b)(2), and 8(b)(4)(A).

STATE FULL-CREW LAWS

Governmental support of featherbedding is apparent in state full-crew laws. Originally enacted to reduce accidents and increase safety, the laws have served mainly to increase employment of brakemen, although they usually fix the manning requirements for the other operating crafts, too.

The number of brakemen required is determined by the
length of the train and the steepness of track grades. The
railroads have fought hard for repeal of these laws in the
past two decades, on the grounds that conditions have
changed drastically and large crews are no longer necessary. Air brakes, automatic switching, block signal systems,
double tracks, hot box detectors, centralized traffic control
equipment, and improved rolling stock have reduced the
need for brakemen whose number specified in these laws
is related to the time when their tasks included running
along the top of moving box cars to set or release hand
brakes. Their main job today is not to work brakes but
rather to watch for sources of damage or accident to the
train. Modern air brakes are controlled from the cab by an
engineer who is in radio communication with a conductor
in the caboose. The question of safety has lost much of its
validity as a factor in the employment of brakemen. Nevertheless, unions contend that heavier trains require more employees to reduce physical strain and minimize accidents.

Full-crew laws generally provide that the train crew
shall include an engineer, conductor, fireman, and one or
more brakemen (depending on the length of the train),
but these laws vary considerably among the states; and some
of them are comparatively weak and ineffective. About sixteen states have such statutes in effect. These include Arizona, Arkansas, California, Indiana, Maine, Massachusetts,
Mississippi, Nebraska, Nevada, New York, North Dakota,
Ohio, Oregon, Texas, Washington, and Wisconsin. In seven
additional states—including Connecticut, Louisiana, Michigan, New Jersey, Pennsylvania, Rhode Island, and West
Virginia—statutes provide that the size of the crew shall be
determined by a state commission; and in three states—
Connecticut, Louisiana, and Michigan—the appropriate
agency has acted. All the laws are allegedly based on the
need for efficient and safe operation of the railroad system,
but, with one exception, they were enacted before 1920.

Although the full-crew laws were upheld by the United States Supreme Court on several occasions, beginning in 1911,[35] such legislation was declared unconstitutional by the Supreme Court of Pennsylvania in 1939 because it places arbitrary and unreasonable requirements on the railroads and the public and has no tendency to promote safety.[36] The railroad brotherhoods, ordinarily effective lobbyists in Washington, D. C., were unsuccessful in their efforts to obtain federal full-crew laws in 1932, 1934, 1935, and 1937. They also failed in the recent postwar period to include such provisions in collective bargaining agreements.

Engineers and firemen have been more concerned with train-limit laws since all operating crafts are favorably affected by such legislation. Four states—Arizona, Louisiana, Oklahoma, and Nevada—have passed laws which limit the number of cars in railroad trains, though Congress rejected pressures for similar action a number of times in the 1930's.[37] During World War II, the Interstate Commerce Commission suspended the train-limit statutes for the duration of the emergency as a waste of human and capital resources but the full-crew laws were not eased. In 1945, the United States Supreme Court held the Arizona law unconstitutional because it had no reasonable relation to safety.[38] Since then train-limit laws have not been enforced. Union arguments that safety is enhanced by full-crew and train-limit laws have not been borne out. State utility commissions with discretion to fix the size of train crews have not required the minimum manning arrangements set forth in typical state laws. It also has generally been the best judgment that longer and fewer freight trains provide more safety than a greater number of shorter ones.

Thirteen states have laws that require firemen on diesel locomotives, but five of these laws apply only to road service. Although several more states authorize their public utility commissions to require firemen on diesels, no such orders have been issued. In 1960 there were seven cities in six states which had enacted municipal ordinances requiring firemen on locomotives.

Some of the states with full-crew laws have been under union and carrier pressures to enact modifications. A California law passed in 1911 specified the number of brakemen that freight trains must carry; seven was the maximum required, depending on conditions. In 1948 the voters of the state approved by a narrow margin an amendment to allow the Public Utilities Commission to determine the number of brakemen required on freight trains to promote the safety of employees, passengers, and the public. One clause states that ". . . the Commission shall not require employment of such number of brakemen as will result in featherbed practices." [39] The railroads estimated that savings would be about $3,000,000. Subsequent regulations by the Commission greatly reduced the number of brakemen used. In 1959 California amended the law to require employment of firemen on diesel locomotives. The same year, Wisconsin extended its full-crew law, previously applicable only to steam-operated railroads, to diesel-powered trains.

It is clear that the railroads cannot easily bring about abrogation of the state laws. An attempt to repeal the Arkansas full-crew law by popular referendum failed in 1926 and a similar effort was defeated in 1958 when about fifty-seven percent of those voting cast ballots against the proposal. The railroad companies had urged that the third brakeman was no longer necessary for safe operation of the trains and that his elimination would save $3,000,000 annually. Voters apparently saw the issue mainly in terms of loss of jobs.

A special report submitted to the governor of New York in 1959 on problems of the railroad lines recommended that the state Public Service Commission (PSC) be permitted to authorize variations in the state full-crew law.[40] The state legislature directed the PSC to investigate the matter. (The New York law requires a crew of five or six men, depending upon the number of cars in the train; engines without cars must have three men.) The Public Service Commission held hearings at which the carriers charged that the statute was responsible for the employment of 2,242 unnecessary firemen, brakemen, and baggagemen at a cost of about $14,700,-000 a year. The PSC pointed out, however, that the carriers did recognize that the jobs of 1,598 of these men, receiving $10,300,000 in wages, were protected by labor contracts. At most, only 644 workers, receiving $4,400,000 a year, were employed solely because of the law. The PSC unanimously agreed early in 1960 that the full-crew law was wrong in principle, had no reasonable relationship to safety of operations, and should be repealed so that flexible administrative regulation of crew composition would be possible.[41] Other support for changing the full-crew law in order to reduce operating costs of the railroads came in the report made late in 1960 by the fifteen-man New York State Temporary Commission on Economic Expansion.[42] But legislative bills to effectuate this change were not politically palatable to the legislature, and committees having jurisdiction in the matter did not act. Some of the delay was occasioned by the state attorney general, who raised questions regarding the constitutionality of the law. At the beginning of 1964, however, Governor Nelson A. Rockefeller recommended repeal of the state full-crew law to the legislature.

Railroads maintain that safety on freight trains require no more than four men—an engineer, a conductor, and two brakemen. Unions say that a fireman and third brakeman also are necessary to minimize dangerous conditions. In states which have full-crew laws, however, where five or six men are used, safety records are no better. Bizarre situations are numerous under the diverse state laws.[43] Freight trains leaving Minnesota add a third brakeman through North Dakota. He then leaves and the train passes through Montana and Idaho. At Washington, another brakeman joins the two on the train. Erie-Lackawanna freight trains from New York slow to ten miles an hour or less as they approach Pennsylvania so that one crew man can get off. Normally, the crew man leaving the train is paid for a full day regardless of the time he spends on the job. For the sixteen miles to the state border of the 120-mile freight run between Corning, New York and Newberry Junction, Pennsylvania, a third brakeman joins the train crew. If no train is returning to his home yard, he is permitted to take a taxi at company expense.

State full-crew laws take precedence over contracts between railroads and unions, and they frequently require even more manpower than the work-rules arrangements in effect. Confusion is increased by local ordinances, enacted by municipalities, fixing the size and type of crew required within city limits. Operating costs are increased by different statutes. Railroads estimate that archaic state full-crew laws add about $74,000,000 and 9,400 workers to the payrolls.

The Presidential Railroad Commission indicated a need to repeal the full-crew laws which had failed to keep abreast of modern railroad operations. The Interstate Commerce Commission concluded that revision of state full-crew laws would help significantly to solve the passenger-train deficit problem.[44] The industry, however, may seek federal legislation to remove the power of states to control the size of crews and, thereby, eliminate the very difficult task of seeking repeal of the laws on a state-by-state basis.

OTHER STATE LAWS

State laws dealing with featherbedding, other than those concerning railroad full-crew matters, have been weak and unclear. State actions and experiences have been almost haphazard. Important positive conclusions, therefore, are not evident. Occasionally, the common law has been used to prevent restrictive union practices. Scattered and sundry court decisions have been reached in New York, New Jersey, California, and Wisconsin.[45]

Colorado specifically prohibits coercing employers to hire standby or unneeded workers. Several states make it an unfair labor practice for workers to oppose the installation and use of labor-saving machinery. Pertinent state statutes, including antitrust laws, have been enacted in several instances, but these are of limited scope and have remained untested in the courts. A few more states have criminal statutes which might possibly be applied to cases where restrictive labor practices occur. In a number of situations where state laws do not exist, equity courts have enjoined strikes or picketing to force featherbedding demands on employers.[46]

Chapter VIII

ELIMINATION OF FEATHERBEDDING AND ALLEVIATION OF DISPLACEMENT DISTRESS

The elimination of featherbedding practices is not essentially a legal problem, though blatant activities of this nature by workers and unions must be condemned and prohibited. Efforts by workers to increase job security and employment are at the root of behavior which restricts output and prevents the introduction of labor-saving machinery. Featherbedding will decline as workers lose their fear of technological displacement and feel that new machines represent no threat to their livelihood.

While a solution to the modern problem of labor displacement caused by the introduction of machinery and automation would make featherbedding unnecessary, prospects for successful achievement of this result in the near future are not bright. It is, therefore, necessary to indicate that some significant reduction in makework would probably occur simply by merging the various craft unions of the industries most affected.

Craft union domination of construction, transportation, entertainment, and printing has been responsible in part for the concentration of featherbedding in these industries. Governmental reports have already recommended consolidation of separate unions in the railroad industry and in the airline industry. Similar suggestions are in order for the construction, entertainment, and printing industries, as well. Industrial unions with a more heterogeneous group of workers are less inclined to resist new machines affecting the working opportunities and skills of a small part of the membership, and simultaneously they tend to increase economic security by establishing seniority units on a wider base.

The major attack on featherbedding—preventing its appearance and reducing its existence—must be made by working out ways of assuring workers greater protection against financial insecurity and mental anguish which the loss of a skilled job entails. This kind of approach appears to be the most sensible one.

Some persons are pessimistic about the ability of society to wipe out featherbedding. One student concluded that "the chances are that nothing effective can or will be done about featherbedding. Perhaps most people will have to console themselves by agreeing with Secretary of Labor Mitchell that this practice will probably never spread beyond the four industries in which it is most deeply entrenched— railroading, printing, music, and construction—and that automation will save the situation before it gets out of hand." [1] It is more likely, however, that slow progress will be made in eradicating makework.

DISPLACEMENT OF LABOR

As soon as it became evident that labor-saving machinery caused displacement, methods of alleviating the impact on workers were suggested. Jean B. Say, who was one of the first to analyze the problem systematically, felt that adverse effects might be minimized if new machinery were restricted to areas where labor was in short supply. The use of the new machinery should be spread gradually, governmental public works should be planned for the employment of those made idle, and populations should be shifted from one region to another as circumstances warrant.[2]

During the past two centuries, many individuals and various groups have espoused reversion by society to more primitive forms of production and the abandonment of much of the prevailing machine technology. It is true that a few persons, including Oswald Spengler, were more concerned to arrest the declining role of the landed aristocracy, but others, like William Morris and Mohandas K. Gandhi, were concerned about the effects of the machine on joblessness for some workers and in its effects on the pride and pleasure in the nature and creativity of work for many others who retained employment. There have been serious proposals for putting a moratorium on invention, and Congress has been asked to prohibit the issuance of patents on labor-saving devices. Such techniques, however, are too remote from possibilities of realistic implementation.

For a long time some persons have contended that a reduction in the hours of work would increase the number of jobs available. Unions in particular have taken this position and have striven in various ways to bring about shorter hours. Historically, union policies aimed first for shorter work days and later shifted emphasis to shorter work weeks, but other methods for contracting hours of work have been used. For example, negotiations which substantially lengthened the period of vacation in the steel and aluminum industries have recently been successfully concluded. Generally, employers oppose reductions in the standard work week. The federal government, too, currently is against shorter hours because it believes that economic growth will be curbed.

From the very beginning of its existence, the American Federation of Labor has maintained that shorter hours is a paramount palliative for reducing unemployment resulting from the introduction of machinery. In 1887 the convention of the AFL declared that the evil of unemployment resulting from the introduction of machinery can be met only by reducing the hours of labor. The campaign for shorter hours persisted at succeeding conventions. In 1907 the annual convention unanimously supported a report by a special committee which said in part: " . . . in those trades in which the development of machinery is making such wonderful strides, it is absolutely necessary that the hours of work be shortened, in order that the opportunities for employment may be shared by all members." [3] This attitude still dominates the thinking of the labor movement.

Yet the effects of a cut in hours (while maintaining weekly earnings) are not clear. If hours are reduced, the tendency is for output to fall, the rate of growth to decline, and prices to rise. Employers are more inclined under those circumstances to undertake technological advance, and it is possible that even fewer jobs might be the result. Furthermore, if more hours of work are necessary, employers might prefer using the staff they already have, at overtime rates, rather than take on new men. New employees are more likely to be less skilled and, although not paid overtime rates, they burden employers with additional fringe benefits such as pension contributions, paid vacations and holidays, and health and welfare protection costs. Unions with manning rules and rigid apprenticeship clauses in their contracts often do not want to provide more men for extra shifts but prefer overtime payments to existing jobholders. The overall effects of a reduction of working hours on employment is not clear.

The task of providing jobs for the technologically displaced during the next few years is part of a larger problem because the economy must simultaneously absorb the many hundreds of thousands of young workers who complete their education and join the labor force each year and the four million persons who are currently idle. Workers displaced by automation, however, are receiving the most attention.

The greatest impact of technological advance on employment has been in agriculture. During the past century, agricultural employment has fallen from fifty to ten percent of the labor force; in the past fifty years even the absolute number of workers on farms has declined. As this downward trend continues, an occupational shift is taking place among those who remain in the industry. Farm laborers are becoming knowledgeable machinists, and the farmer must learn biochemistry.

But it has been in connection with the displacement of manufacturing workers that the greatest concern has been expressed. Recent technological change has caused much disemployment, that is, a decline in employment resulting from higher productivity. Between 1953 and 1959, 1,131,000 production workers in manufacturing were disemployed. Rising productivity eliminated the jobs of at least 200,000 factory workers each year from 1957 through 1961. Elsewhere in the economy, many more were released by industry; still others will lose their jobs in the years ahead. It has been estimated that 200,000 or more workers in nonagricultural industries will be disemployed each year during the next decade.[4] Since many workers without skills are not rehired, the number of long-term unemployed has risen sharply over the past decade. Much of the displacement problem falls on poorly educated and poorly trained persons.

Protection against the impact of displacement may be instituted by unilateral action of employers, collective bargaining arrangements, or governmental legislation and programs. There are many old techniques and devices which may be modified somewhat to suit the immediate problems under consideration. Some of these techniques and devices have played a part in assisting workers unemployed for reasons other than technological change. New ideas also have been developed and are being used to ease the transition of displaced workers to new jobs or into retirement. It is important to recognize that implementing and financing programs linked to technological unemployment rather than cyclical unemployment is easier because in the former case the company is not financially pressed. On the contrary, introduction of new machines is designed to yield a saving in costs.

Various private and governmental programs to meet the needs of displaced workers, sometimes currently considered alternatives for one another, might best be used as supplements if properly integrated. Undoubtedly this procedure would increase the short-run total costs of employers for supporting technologically displaced workers. Yet, otherwise employers are faced with resistance to the introduction of new technology and the costs of retaining workers who are not required. Providing reasonable financial protection for displaced workers therefore seems to be a sound approach. Employers, however, must now carefully consider potential costs of technological displacement, when deciding whether to hire new workers.

Amelioration of the effects of displacement requires careful study and thorough planning. In the 1930's an examination of the problem of technological advance was made by a group of experts. It was found that the interval from the making of an invention to the time its social effects become evident is about thirty years.[5] Although there has been some contraction in the time period since then, the gap represents the interval during which something must be done if effective action is to be taken.

Employers should consult with the unions and employees involved and give them advance notice of intended changes in machinery and equipment. This procedure allows workers time to look for other jobs and put their financial affairs in order; it enables unions to make recommendations which they consider to be justified; and it permits the community to gear itself to the impending change and provide what assistance it can to ease the transitional pains experienced by displaced workers.

The strongest unions strive to maintain jobs and earnings. If the union has built up a series of work rules dealing with manning, work loads, and conditions under which new equipment may be introduced, it is in a position to trade them for other substantial benefits. But this situation is not frequent among unions. Many of them are too weak to gain full protection for their members against technological displacement. As a result, unions generally must seek more limited arrangements, such as severance pay, moving expenses, restrictions on relocating plants, guaranteed wages or employment, advance notice of displacement, retraining allowances, supplementary unemployment benefits, and early retirement arrangements for those whose jobs are discontinued. Some of the bitter bargaining relationships

connected with these issues have been eased by developing
new techniques such as using neutral persons, avoiding
fixed contract termination dates, and continuing the bargaining process and sessions even after the agreement has
been signed.

Generally, advancing technology requires policies that
protect the jobs of workers or provide financial arrangements
that enable those who are displaced to assume the economic
burdens they face. One of the sensible and widely accepted
compromise solutions is to do away with the job but
insulate the jobholder from adverse economic effects. A
policy of attrition is a transitional device which protects
the worker rather than the job. Employees holding a job
at a particular time are kept on the payroll till retirement,
death, disability, discharge, resignation, promotion, or
transfer occurs or for a predetermined period. But they
are not replaced. Simultaneously, older workers may be
required to retire. Although a policy of attrition under which
regular employees are secure from job losses consequent
upon technological change is sound, it is not always possible
to differentiate clearly between displacement caused by
technology and job losses caused by cyclical and seasonal
variations in demand.

The cost of an attrition program to an employer depends
on the alternative arrangements available to him, the age
distribution of the employees involved, and the use to which
the retained workers are put. Union objections to a policy
of attrition arise from the likelihood that this approach will
lead to a reduction of its economic power at the bargaining table and its political power in governmental councils.

ATTEMPTS BY INDUSTRY TO EASE DISPLACEMENT

Private enterprise must assume even more responsibility
than it has in mitigating the effects of technological displacement. New approaches and accommodations between
managerial flexibility and job security need to be sought and
found. Thus far the main efforts of employers have been

concentrated on intracompany transfers, retraining, severance pay, seniority arrangements, supplemental unemployment benefits, and early retirement provisions.

Transfer to other jobs in the plant, whether with or without retraining, is one way of reducing distress. The wages of workers shifted to jobs requiring less skill should decline, yet often this does not happen. Workers may continue to receive the same wage rates previously earned at the company. Such payments, called red circle or incumbent rates, are made to enable a worker to maintain his morale and his accustomed standard of living. Since these payments are contrary to the principle of equal pay for equal work, workers who receive them often are not given the wage advances received by other workers until all rates have fallen in line. Operating railroad workers were very critical of the Presidential Railroad Commission for disregarding the red circle principle.[6]

Companies with more than one plant are sometimes in a better position to transfer workers. As yet, very few collective bargaining agreements provide for the interplant transfer of displaced employees at multiplant companies. When provision for transfer is made, employees may be entitled to preferential hiring at other plants, an opportunity to be shifted with the operation, or bumping rights at other plants. Decisions by employees as to whether to move or not have depended on the geographical distance separating the plants, seniority status acquired at the new plant, the comparability of the positions available, and moving allowances.[7] To a very limited extent, payments for moving and readjustment expenses to workers who are required to change their residence have been included in collective bargaining agreements.

Until the past few years, the task of training and retraining workers was primarily a function of private enterprise. Companies finding their labor supply inadequate undertook to teach workers particular skills. Some of the craft unions, such as electricians, lithographers, plumbers, and printers have collaborated with employers in carrying out the training function.

Public attention has been focused on the need for retraining technologically displaced workers for a long time. A comprehensive analysis of the problem was made at a symposium in 1930 in which some leading scholars participated, including Sumner H. Slichter, Paul H. Douglas, Rexford G. Tugwell, Isador Lubin, Stuart Chase, and Charles A. Beard.[8] In 1940 a government report stated: "Retraining of workers whose occupations had become modified or obsolete as a result of technological changes is assuming increasing importance in programs designed to reduce displacement to a minimum. Minor modifications in specific operations have taken place continually in all occupations. In such instances retraining has been carried on in practically all industrial establishments, either through expert demonstrations, observations of one worker by another, or through organized training supplementary to actual performance on the job. However, where technological changes had eliminated an operation entirely and a new one had been substituted in its place . . . transfer of workers to the new jobs required more fundamental retraining. Similar training has been necessary where transfer to different operations was attempted. Such retraining in some instances has been undertaken by trade-unions, by employers, or by both in cooperative schools." [9]

Even if it costs more to retrain workers than to hire new ones, the task generally should be done in order to maintain the morale of those employed. Retraining workers may require the combined resources of the community. Employers must give as much advance warning of technological displacement as possible to allow other appropriate groups and governmental units to function properly. Industry, labor unions, government, and the school system all have a role to play in working out retraining programs. Some workers are not interested in being retrained. But lack of basic and elementary education—inability to read, write, and comprehend simple relationships—is one of the major obstacles in retraining workers. Large numbers of illiterates are not qualified for retraining at costs which employers consider reasonable.

The importance of basic education in retraining is clearly illustrated by an experience at Inland Steel Company. An officer said that "in setting up qualifications for jobs in the new galvanizing processes, the ability to speak, read and write English and do simple arithmetical calculations became a requirement for the first time. This requirement was imposed by the fact that the new process puts the men at considerable physical distances from each other, whereas formerly the men worked within conversational range. Workers unable to understand the foreman's orders could get them interpreted by fellow workers. Today, all communication within the galvanizing department is either by intercom or by written memorandum. Consequently, twenty percent of the men employed in the old galvanizing operation were ineligible for jobs on the new process: they could not meet these new qualifications." [10]

Older workers who are laid off have greater difficulty than younger persons in finding new jobs and need particularly good training programs. A study made by the Bureau of Labor Statistics of the United States Department of Labor found that older workers who had continued to improve the level of their educational attainments as they advanced in years are retrained more successfully. It is also beneficial if older workers receive counseling prior to entering a retraining project. The study concluded "that age, by itself, is not a reliable or useful criterion for determining the suitability of workers for retraining." [11] Individual capacity and aptitudes are more important than chronological age.

Severance pay or dismissal wages is an old device, dating back to the early 1920's, which is used to help tide an employee over a period of unemployment following termination of his job. In part, it is considered payment for loss of job rights, such as seniority and pension. It offers a certain amount of special protection to employees because it en-

courages employers to transfer rather than permanently
lay off workers, even if there are retraining costs. Dismissal wages are usually given in the form of a lump sum
when permanent layoff, discharge, or resignation occurs,
and are paid in addition to wages, accumulated vacation,
and other benefits due at the time. About a quarter of all
union agreements provide for severance pay. Typically, one
week's wages is provided for each year of service.

Severance pay is one of the provisions unions seek for
technologically displaced workers. Although it can serve
only to provide assistance for a relatively short period, it is
intended to be used in conjunction with other efforts to
help workers who need new employment opportunities to
readjust. It is, therefore, unfortunate that about a third of
the states disqualify recipients of severance pay from unemployment compensation benefits.

The principle of seniority assures workers of a degree of
job tenure which depends upon the length of time they
have been employed by a firm and eliminates some possible
arbitrary action by employers when making layoffs. But the
benefit to many employees may be small, and sometimes
they prefer alternative arrangements. As a result, beginning
in the 1890's some companies unilaterally and others through
collective bargaining adopted various forms of annual employment or income guarantees. Usually only establishments having relatively stable production schedules are
willing to undertake such plans. And even then the guarantee is limited to regular rather than temporary employees.
These programs have not been frequent in American industry. In a way, they represent the forerunner of supplemental
unemployment benefits.

Supplemental unemployment benefits (SUB) may assist
some workers who have been technologically displaced.
The plan was introduced in 1955 in the automobile industry as a result of a drive by the automobile workers' union
for guaranteed wages. It has not been widely adopted
because workers adequately protected by seniority provi-

sions gain little from SUB and prefer to have other benefits negotiated for them. Plans currently in effect cover about 2,000,000 workers and are largely confined to manufacturing industries producing automobiles, automobile parts, basic steel, rubber, cans, and glass, and the maritime industry.

SUB provide company supplements to state unemployment compensation (UC) benefits through a pooled-fund or individual-account system for periods ranging from about thirty-nine to fifty-two weeks. Usually, the object is to bring combined SUB and UC payments to about two-thirds of the wages of those employed. Only two states have refused to make unemployment compensation payments available to those receiving supplemental unemployment benefits. Generally, however, integration of these programs has been achieved. In a few cases, SUB have also been linked with severance pay.

Making early retirement for workers more attractive helps to alleviate the adverse effects of technological change on older employees who become eligible to retire as well as on those who are able to retain their jobs because others have retired. Presently, the federal old age, survivors, and disability insurance (OASDI) program defeats this purpose by paying lower benefits to persons retiring at sixty-two than to those retiring at sixty-five years of age. Other conditions which reduce the disposition of persons to retire early and should be modified include disqualification from unemployment compensation to OASDI recipients by some states and to those getting private pensions by an even larger number of states. While plans for earlier retirement increase the costs employers must bear, such outlays should be offset against costs of supporting larger unemployment programs or keeping unnecessary workers on the payroll.

Collective bargaining agreements to establish funds and provide certain benefits to technologically displaced and unemployed workers are being used with increasing frequency by employers and unions. The purpose and type of provisions regulating the operations of a fund may encourage or discourage further technological advance. For example, if payments by employers are geared to output, there is less incentive for employers to automate than if they are based on man-hours of labor. On the other hand, employee cooperation in pushing technological change would also depend on the method of financing a fund. Funds may have the objective of sharing the gains of change with workers, maintenance of job and income security, protecting job and benefit rights of retained employees, and compensating displaced workers for the loss of such rights. Better labor and public relations may follow establishment of a fund which encourages industrial harmony.

Funds created by collective bargaining may be used to benefit retained employees or displaced workers. Thus far, emphasis has been put on benefits to those workers who retain their jobs after technological advance occurs. Employers tend to favor this approach because they want to secure effective work performance from the employees who remain with them, and the unions, for internal political reasons, need to improve conditions for jobholders and active members rather than for those who are being detached from the industry. Yet the key problems of technological change and automation concern displaced workers, and more provision will have to be made for this group in the future. Various categories of benefits have been created, including assistance in finding new employment by providing retraining, moving expenses, and improved employment service; maintaining the income of displaced workers during the period between jobs or improving severance pay; and continuation of health and welfare benefits. Some attention has been given to providing earlier retirement opportunities and vesting of pension rights.

SOME SPECIFIC ILLUSTRATIONS

A variety of joint union and management committees and programs have been established to study the impact of technology on manpower. Many of them are routine and perfunctory. A few have sought the help of experts and are adequately financed. Joint labor-management committees continue to meet on a year-round basis seeking solutions to problems of technological displacement in the steel, rubber, meatpacking, electrical manufacturing, coal, construction, maritime, and other industries.

Coal

In 1923, the United States Coal Commission reported that there was some opposition to the introduction of machinery in the bituminous coal mining industry, particularly at the local level. The officers of the national union repeatedly went on record in favor of new machinery, but they demanded that workers receive a share of the resultant savings. At the local level, however, there was fear that the use of machinery would increase the irregularity of work. To prevent the introduction of machinery, locals struck or more frequently failed to agree on wage rates for operators of the new equipment.[12] Limitation of output was also found in the anthracite coal mining industry.[13]

One of the first major efforts to deal with displacement through establishment of a jointly administered employer-employee fund was made in the bituminous coal industry. The introduction of new equipment and greater management efficiency greatly increased productivity of labor during the past two decades. The union has encouraged mechanization and has made no attempt to featherbed or retain jobs which are unnecessary. The decline in employment has been great and the trend of average annual hours for those working has been downward for a score of years. The fund, however, is not especially geared to help those miners whose jobs are eliminated. All miners, including those displaced, are eligible for pensions, hospital and medical care, funeral expenses, and payments to their widows and survivors. Coal mining areas have become generally depressed and chronic unemployment has prevailed, but rapid mechanization has enabled the industry to survive.

Oil Refining

The prospects of the successful introduction of new technology or the elimination of obsolete work rules are increased if workers are carefully prepared in advance. An effort to change work rules at a British oil refining subsidiary of the Standard Oil Company of New Jersey terminated favorably. This result was possible because the company is not part of an industrywide bargaining group, has had good labor relations in the past, was willing to absorb losses during the first stages of reorganization, and sold the plan to the workers in a prolonged period of education and indoctrination. The union agreed to eliminate the jobs of large numbers of helpers, reduce tea breaks and clean-up time, and liberalize rigid demarcations in work assignments. In return, wages were increased so that pay for forty hours now exceeds what was previously earned in fifty. All workers whose jobs were eliminated were retrained in an extensive program and no dismissals or layoffs took place. Changes in the rules enabled the company to add forty percent to its plant capacity without increasing the work force. Productivity has risen and flexibility of work schedules has increased.[14]

Automation Equipment

Joint management-union study of displacement problems has been undertaken with increasing frequency in this industry as a result of collective bargaining. United States Industries, a manufacturer of automation equipment, has established the Foundation on Automation and Employment to study the impact of technological change on the worker. A joint sponsor of the project is the International Association of Machinists, the main representative of the company's production employees. Operating revenues come from contributions made by the company based on the price at which it sells or leases equipment.

Meatpacking

Another approach to the problem of changing technology where automation is expected to reduce the work force permanently has been provided in the agreements negotiated in 1959 between Armour and Company and the two major meatpacking unions covering 14,000 production and maintenance workers in twenty-six plants.[15] Reduced employment opportunities brought on by mechanization and new methods of production and displacement caused by locational shifts in the industry and the growth of smaller packing houses are studied by a joint committee, headed by an impartial chairman. The committee administers an automation fund made up of company contributions based on the weight of product shipped from its plants. The maximum contribution by Armour during the two-year contract period was set at $500,000. The money is used to study problems resulting from the modernization program of the company and to pay for any training authorized by the joint committee. The agreement puts emphasis on training employees to perform new and changed jobs and planning interplant transfers in those instances where job opportunities are available. The primary purpose of the fund, however, is to investigate displacement problems rather than pay benefits to workers.

In the middle of 1961, the committee reported that the resources of management and labor available for solving the employment problems caused by technological change were very inadequate for the purpose and that government help would be necessary.[16] It discussed the pilot retraining and pilot transfer programs set up in connection with the closing of the Oklahoma City plant.

Most of the money in the fund had not yet been spent when the contract expired. Under the new agreement reached in 1961, Armour compensates workers who are displaced when plants close, if they agree to transfer, with supplemental unemployment compensation payments for up to thirty-nine weeks. Relocation costs chargeable to the automation fund are also provided. But the 1961 contract discontinued company payments into the fund.[17]

In August, 1963, one of the two unions involved charged that the plan was ineffective and merely served to provide publicity for the company. The president of the packinghouse workers said: "Since the formation of the automation committee, Armour has closed down at least one plant in each and every year. For very few, if any, of the 3,200 workers thus displaced has an employment provision been made by Armour." [18] The company countered with information that of 1,160 workers affected by the closing of the Sioux City, Iowa, plant in June, 1963, 797 requested and received separation pay; 114 retired with pensions; and 249 requested transfers to other plants. It added that 158 workers were placed and forty-two more were awaiting transfer to jobs already reserved. The meat cutters and butcher workmen union, the other labor union involved, has been satisfied with the operation of the plan.

Steel

One of the more interesting developments during the steel strike of 1959-1960 was the signing of a separate agreement between Kaiser Steel Corporation and the steelworkers' union. The company broke away from the other struck firms and worked out an understanding. A joint committee was established to study the problems of work rules, automation, and technological change and to make recommendations. A second committee, which included public members, was created to work out a long-range plan for equitable sharing of the gains of the company's progress. In practice, the second committee has taken over the functions of the first.

Kaiser and the union set up a committee of three public, three company, and three union representatives. The incentive system in effect was criticized by the company and workers for its inequities and ineffectiveness. Grievances and other dissatisfactions led the committee to devise a new scheme to protect workers from losses due to new machinery or improved work methods and provide them with a greater stake in higher productivity of the plant. However, the program emphasizes savings in costs rather than increases in output. Under the plan, workers receive 32.5 percent of the difference between a standardized cost of producing steel and the actual cost. About sixty percent of production and maintenance workers are covered by the arrangement, and since March, 1963 they have received supplementary monthly payments.[19] The amount received by each worker depends on the degree of his skill. The other forty percent of the company's employees are still working under the incentive plan, but they may shift to the savings sharing plan if they think they will gain that way.

Men displaced by machines are put in a plantwide employment reserve labor pool. Remuneration and seniority continue during this period. These workers are given any jobs available in the plant as they open up, even if retraining is necessary to qualify them. They also are used to fill in for absentees or produce items which the company ordinarily buys from other firms.

GOVERNMENT PROGRAMS

It is generally agreed that the government will have to participate in financial arrangements to ease the displacement effects because of the huge costs involved. "The real problem created by technological change is . . . one of the most acute of our contemporary legislative problems of social security—a matter which cannot be handled adequately without all of society helping to finance, presumably through some sort of taxation, a displacement wage, a retraining period and a replacement program. For if the consuming public benefits by technological development, as it undoubtedly does, then it should share the burden of paying for such benefits and not leave the social cost almost entirely on the shoulders of displaced wage earners and their families. Indeed, a perfectly valid argument justifying our courts in refusing to interfere with techno-

logical strikes of any kind is the effect such strikes might
have in accelerating the type of legislation mentioned above.
After our legislatures have in this way obviated the disas-
trous immediate effects of technological progress, then, and
only then, will even they be in a position to make technological strikes unlawful." [20]

One of the main tasks assigned to the twenty-one member
tripartite President's Advisory Committee on Labor-Management Policy created in February, 1961 was consideration of
the problems created by automation and other technological
advances. The Committee has been seeking ways of assuring the maximum possible growth of the economy without
concomitantly incurring significant or lasting unemployment.
The Committee feels that the highest practicable rate of
economic growth, which is dependent on technological
advance, is the best assurance of full employment, general
welfare, and national economic strength. Nevertheless, special employment policies are called for during periods of
rapid technological change. These policies depend upon a
combination of governmental and private action taken
within the framework of a free society. Improved vocational
education and retraining programs, modification in unemployment compensation plans to encourage retraining, and
facilitating labor mobility by sharing costs of moving and
retraining, protecting seniority and pension rights, and minimizing the human problems involved are the major needs
for safeguarding against economic injury to individuals and
successful adaptation and adjustment to change.[21]

The impact of technological displacement is alleviated by
governmental programs which reduce other types of unemployment. Cyclical changes in employment are subject
to governmental monetary and fiscal policies. Seasonal and
irregular unemployment require both public and private
action to regularize business operations as far as possible,
but their effects on workers are eased by unemployment
compensation and the work of public employment offices.
Secular declines in industry necessitate retraining workers
whose skills have become obsolete so they can shift to other

occupations. This is particularly true in light of the fact that some alternative arrangements, such as agreements to keep an excessive number of employees on a job temporarily, have a tendency to become permanent and reduce the efficiency of production. The most important governmental programs which assist technologically unemployed workers provide unemployment compensation and retraining.

Unemployment compensation or unemployment insurance currently provides the main source of financial protection for technologically unemployed persons. Since the late 1930's unemployed workers willing and able to accept suitable jobs have been eligible to receive benefits for a period of twenty-six weeks or longer. These benefits are paid by the states under a federally coordinated program. Unemployment compensation was originally conceived as a short-term device to cushion a worker between jobs by providing him with about fifty percent of his former wages. The actual proportion of average weekly wages received by unemployed workers typically is somewhat less.

Since persons must be available for work to draw benefits, most states bar payment to those undertaking retraining education. It seems advisable to modify this kind of provision to permit technologically displaced workers being retrained for other employment to retain eligibility for UC payments. But other sources of financial support must also be available to safeguard the standards of those displaced persons who are likely to undergo more prolonged unemployment.

Federal legislation to develop skills in the work force was first enacted in 1917 with passage of the Smith-Hughes Vocational Education Act. This law was subsequently expanded on several occasions. The federal government agreed to aid the states financially in providing agricultural, home economics, and industrial education if the state vocational education program met specified standards. An interesting training provision which has not been utilized effectively was passed in 1937. That year, the Railroad Unemployment

Insurance Act authorized the Railroad Retirement Board
to set up training programs for the prevention and reduction of unemployment. Little has been done in this connection by the Railroad Retirement Board, however.[22] In the
mid-1950's, with unemployment once again a serious problem, several states initiated training programs for persons
without jobs. Massachusetts, Michigan, Ohio, Pennsylvania,
Connecticut, and West Virginia undertook to prepare workers for new employment under differing plans and arrangements. The success of these programs varied, but in all
cases very few persons benefited.

The federal government recently has shown much more
interest in retraining persons whose skills are obsolete. It
has enacted two laws designed to qualify workers for new
employment and to assist them financially while they are
being so prepared. The first of these statutes is the Area
Redevelopment Act of 1961[23] administered by the Area
Redevelopment Administration (ARA) of the Department
of Commerce. The statute encourages the building of factories and facilities that increase employment in depressed
areas. The ARA is authorized to lend a company or governmental unit up to sixty-five percent of the cost of an
industrial or rural redevelopment project for the purchase
and development of land and the erection and improvement
of factories. It can lend up to 100 percent of the cost
of construction of a public facility. The law authorizes
the Secretaries of Labor, Agriculture, and Health, Education,
and Welfare to consult and set up vocational training programs in redevelopment areas for unemployed workers, including farm laborers. Costs of retraining or training workers
are borne by the ARA. Subsistence allowances equal to the
average amount paid under unemployment compensation in
the state are available for a maximum of sixteen weeks to
those being trained for new jobs. In 1963, areas inhabited
by about a fifth of the population were classified as depressed.

The second federal law bears even more directly on displacement problems. The Manpower Development and

Training Act of 1962[24] is designed to retrain those whose skills are made obsolete by technological change and to help those who have no skills. The type of training offered is based on labor market surveys, made by the Department of Labor, of the skills needed by industry. The training program is carried out mainly in vocational schools operated by existing state agencies under the supervision of the Department of Health, Education, and Welfare, but on-the-job training conducted by employers, states, or other public and private agencies is also possible. Workers selected must be unable to secure full-time employment without such training, have had three years of work experience, have passed the age of twenty-one, and be heads of households. Trainees receive allowances comparable to state unemployment compensation benefits for periods up to fifty-two weeks. Smaller allowances are made to young persons or those without work experience. It was estimated that the three-year program should provide retraining for about 400,000 workers and limited on-the-job training to about 250,000 more. The vastness of this training program overshadows the one created by the Area Redevelopment Act.

Travel and moving expenses are often important in giving an unemployed worker mobility and inducing him to take a job. Yet neither the Area Redevelopment Act nor the Manpower Development and Training Act makes provision for relocation allowances. Thus far, only limited influence has been exercised by the government on problems of moving workers or determining the location of private plants.

The Trade Expansion Act of 1962[25] does not deal with problems of displacement by machinery, but it has a point of special interest because, unlike the area redevelopment and manpower development laws, it provides for lump-sum relocation expenses. It also authorizes federally supported readjustment allowances for up to seventy-eight weeks to participants of training programs who lose their jobs as a result of lower tariffs negotiated under the law. About

90,000 workers could be affected during the five-year period
in which the statute is effective.

SOME CONCLUSIONS

Featherbedding by workers has generally been an out-
growth of the process of technological change. Its occur-
rence in the transportation industries—railroads, airlines,
trucking, and shipping—invariably has been associated with
mechanical advance. To a large extent, makework practices
in the construction and printing industries have also been
related to mechanical progress. Although featherbedding
policies among musicians were by and large developed independently of technological modifications in the industry,
they were neither vigorously nor uniformly enforced until
displacement became a problem. The development of
featherbedding in American industry can be traced to
technological change.

But featherbedding does not occur in all industries undergoing technological advance. Nor does its appearance
depend on the rate of mechanical advance in industry.
Makework has occurred in those sectors of the economy
where craft unions have existed. It has constituted an effort
by unions representing a group of workers with homogene-
ous occupational interests to prevent displacement. Even
more important, it has been an attempt to protect workers
against the loss of skills acquired only after considerable
training and experience. Such has been the situation moti-
vating the unions of construction workers, printers, musicians, and airline employees.

Where unskilled work is involved or when industrial
unionism prevails, featherbedding has generally been nonexistent. For example, despite very rapid advances in the
mechanical techniques of agricultural production, the unskilled status of farm labor has made featherbedding un-
feasible in that industry. Industrial unions predominate in
manufacturing, and makework is extremely rare. The varied
occupational interests of the many workers in such unions
make it economically unsound, from the point of view of

the entire membership, and politically unwise for the leadership to seek to institute featherbedding policies which will benefit only small groups of members.

Solutions to the controversies between management and labor concerning featherbedding are more favorable to the immediate interests of the workers involved to the extent that the industry is more prosperous and the costs of the practices represent a smaller proportion of total operating expenditures. These are among the reasons for the bitterness of the struggle in the railroad industry and for the relatively dormant status of the issue in printing and entertainment.

The problem of featherbedding confronting those engaged in collective bargaining and disturbing the public and its elected officials must be tackled mainly by revising the techniques used to adjust workers to technological change. Many makework practices are less meaningful and desirable to industrial unions than they are to craft unions, and governmental encouragement of craft union mergers and industrial bargaining units is in order. Still, the main impetus for the eradication of featherbedding must come from governmental and private programs which offer workers more job security and greater reassurance against technological displacement. It is certainly clear that private efforts alone are incapable of solving the problems involved.

The economy must put more energy into efforts to deal with technological change. Although unemployment affects younger, older, and Negro workers to a greater extent than the labor force as a whole, and although the incidence of unemployment is not uniform occupationally and industrially, there are special conditions that must be recognized and particular situations that require concerted energies of management and labor along with federal, state, and local governments. For example, marked shifts are taking place in the occupational distribution of the labor force. The United States Department of Labor has estimated that the demand for professional and technical workers will increase by sixty-three percent between 1960 and 1975 even though the total labor force will expand by only thirty-one percent.[26]

Government must accelerate its programs to retrain workers in skills which industry seeks through vocational education and on-the-job arrangements. Governmental employment offices must improve their techniques of acquiring and interchanging knowledge concerning job opportunities throughout the United States and providing the public with that information. Stimulating mobility of labor and capital is of especial importance.[27] Although it is frequently less costly to move men to the jobs, encouraging industry to move to areas where unemployment is heavy instead of locating in regions that have to be built up takes advantage of the existence of facilities such as housing, schools, hospitals, and roads.

But most of all, it is clear that featherbedding and technological displacement will dissolve into insignificance in an economy of full employment where workers have little fear of permanent unemployment. Indeed, under such conditions, European workers have shown no fear of displacement by technology.[28]

NOTES

CHAPTER I

1. Bernhard J. Stern, "Resistances to the Adoption of Technological Innovations," United States National Resources Committee, *Technological Trends and National Policy*, 1937, pp. 39-59.

2. Eric J. Hobsbawm, "The Machine Breakers," *Past & Present*, February, 1952, p. 58.

3. *Ibid.*

4. Sidney Webb and Beatrice Webb, *The History of Trade Unionism*, 1920, p. 88.

5. See *The Parliamentary Debates (Great Britain)*, Volume 21, 1812, pp. 966-72.

6. See chapter 2 of *Shirley*.

7. See *Apex Hosiery Company* v. *Leader*, 310 U.S. 469, 482 (1940).

8. Alfred P. Wadsworth and Julia de L. Mann, *The Cotton Trade and Industrial Lancashire, 1600-1780*, 1931, p. 499.

9. United States Industrial Relations Commission, *Final Report and Testimony*, Volume 1, 1916, p. 768 (testimony of Frederick W. Taylor).

10. Sidney Webb and Beatrice Webb, *Industrial Democracy*, 1920, p. 395.

11. Bernhard J. Stern, *op. cit.*, p. 56.

12. Frank E. Manuel, "The Luddite Movement in France," *The Journal of Modern History*, June, 1938, p. 186.

13. United States Commissioner of Labor, *Eleventh Special Report: Regulation and Restriction of Output*, 1904, p. 921.

14. United States Industrial Commission, *Reports*, Volume 17, 1901, p. lviii.

15. Sidney Webb and Beatrice Webb, *Industrial Democracy*, 1920, pp. 307-09.

16. United States Commissioner of Labor, *op. cit.*, pp. 725-36.

17. Reginald Marriott, *Incentive Payment Systems*, 1957, pp. 138-53. For a discussion of some featherbedding practices in Great Britain, see Colm Brogan, "British Make-Work Takes a Blow," *National Review*, March 28, 1959, pp. 615-16.

18. Eric J. Hobsbawm, *op. cit.*, p. 65.

19. Jean B. Say, *A Treatise on Political Economy*, 1857, p. 87.

20. John Yeats, *The Technical History of Commerce*, 1872, p. 277.

21. Frank E. Manuel, *op. cit.*, p. 211.

22. John Diebold, *Automation: Its Impact on Business and Labor*, 1959, p. 1; John Diebold, *Automation*, 1952, p. 1.

23. John R. Commons, *et al.*, *History of Labour in the United States*, Volume 2, 1918, p. 74.

24. Sumner H. Slichter, *Union Policies and Industrial Management*, 1941, pp. 216-22.

25. George E. Barnett, *Chapters on Machinery and Labor*, 1926, pp. 160-61.

26. Alexander Gourvitch, *Survey of Economic Theory on Technological Change and Employment* (United States Work Projects Administration, National Research Project, Report No. G-6), 1940, pp. v-vi.

27. Eli F. Heckscher, *Mercantilism*, Volume 2, 1935, p. 126.

28. See David Ricardo, *On the Principles of Political Economy and Taxation*, 1821, pp. 466-82.

29. William T. Thornton, *On Labour*, 1869, pp. 316-35.

30. *Ibid.*, pp. 312-13.

31. John S. Mill, "Thornton on Labour and Its Claims," *The Fortnightly Review*, June 1, 1869, pp. 698-99.

32. John E. Cairnes, *Some Leading Principles of Political Economy*, 1874, pp. 249-62.

33. See United States Temporary National Economic Committee, *Investigation of Concentration of Economic Power, Monograph No. 22 (Technology in Our Economy)*, 1941, pp. 37-57.

34. United States Senate Committee on Education and Labor, *Report upon the Relations between Labor and Capital*, Volume 1, 1885, p. 137 and Volume 3, 1885, p. 160.

35. United States Commissioner of Labor, *Thirteenth Annual Report (Hand and Machine Labor, Volume 1)*, 1899, p. 6.

36. There was no apparent concern with the possibility that machines could increase the amount of training and experience necessary to perform a job.

37. United States Industrial Commission, *Final Report*, Volume 19, 1902, pp. 817-27.

38. *Ibid.*, p. 825.

39. United States Commissioner of Labor, *Eleventh Special Report: Regulation and Restriction of Output*, 1904, p. 28.

40. United States Commission on Industrial Relations, *Final Report and Testimony*, Volume 1, 1916, pp. 238-39 (United States Senate, *Document No. 415*, 64th Congress, 1st Session).

41. *Ibid.*, p. 991.

42. Federated American Engineering Societies, Committee on Elimination of Waste in Industry, *Waste in Industry*, 1921, pp. 18-20, 296-98.

43. United States House of Representatives, *Report No. 2685*, 74th Congress, 2nd Session, 1936, p. 1.

44. United States House of Representatives, Subcommittee of the Committee on Labor, *Investigation of Unemployment Caused by Labor-Saving Devices in Industry (Hearings)*, 74th Congress, 2nd Session, 1936, p. 118.

45. *Ibid.*, pp. 52, 56.

CHAPTER II

1. See addenda section to *Webster's New International Dictionary of the English Language* (Second Edition, Unabridged), 1959, p. cix.

2. The fullest discussion of makework and its ramifications appears in Sumner H. Slichter, *Union Policies and Industrial Management*, 1941, pp. 164-281 and Sumner H. Slichter, James J. Healy, and E. Robert Livernash, *The Impact of Collective Bargaining on Management*, 1960, pp. 317-71.

3. Richard L. Tobin, "Let's Get Rid of 'Bogus'—Now!" *Saturday Review*, February 11, 1961, p. 79.

4. *Time*, August 3, 1959, p. 70.

5. *The Economist,* October 6, 1962, p. 62.

6. The American Assembly, Columbia University, *Automation and Technological Change,* 1962, p. 94.

7. Thomas S. Adams and Helen L. Sumner, *Labor Problems,* 1905, pp. 264-65.

8. See, for example, *United States* v. *Bay Area Painters and Decorators Joint Committee,* 49 F.Supp. 733, 737 (1943).

9. 61 Stat. 136, 162 (1947).

10. Sumner H. Slichter, *Union Policies and Industrial Management,* 1941, pp. 165-66.

11. United States Industrial Commission, *Reports,* Volume 17, 1901, p. lix, footnote.

12. Geoffrey Goodman, *Redundancy in the Affluent Society,* 1962, p. 6 (Fabian Tract 340). Redundancy is frequently used interchangeably in Great Britain with unemployment due to layoffs; it refers to workers who are superfluous to the requirements of the employer.

13. Harold J. Laski, "Democracy," *Encyclopaedia of the Social Sciences,* Volume 5, 1931, p. 83; see also *Encyclopaedia Britannica,* Volume 7, 1963, p. 218.

14. John R. Commons, *Legal Foundations of Capitalism,* 1924, pp. 283-88.

15. Selig Perlman, *A Theory of the Labor Movement,* 1928, p. 199.

16. Leon Ardzrooni, "The Philosophy of the Restriction of Output," *The Annals of the American Academy of Political and Social Science,* September, 1920, p. 74.

17. See Kenneth F. Thornbury, "The Crisis on Job Control: A Union View," *Western Business Review,* February, 1960, pp. 35-36. He quotes the idea from the writings of Whiting Williams in the 1920's; see also Arthur R. Porter, Jr., *Job Property Rights: A Study of the Job Controls of the International Typographical Union,* 1954, pp. 7-8 and 75-81 especially.

18. Leon Green, "The Case for the Sit-Down Strike," *The New Republic,* March 24, 1937, p. 199.

19. William Gomberg, "Featherbedding: An Assertion of Property Rights," *The Annals of the American Academy of Political and Social Science,* January, 1961, p. 129.

20. United States House of Representatives, Antitrust Subcommittee of the Committee on the Judiciary, *Current Antitrust Problems, Part 3 (Hearings),* 84th Congress, 1st Session, 1955, p. 2149; see also Arthur J. Goldberg, "Unions and the Antitrust Laws," *Labor Law Journal,* March, 1956, p. 185.

21. *Zdanok* v. *Glidden Company,* 288 F.2d 99, 104, CA 2 (1961); see also 216 F.Supp. 476 (1963).

22. *Oddie* v. *Ross Gear and Tool Company,* 305 F.2d 143, CA 6 (1962).

23. Willard Shelton, "Featherbedding," *New Republic,* July 28, 1947, p. 30.

24. John K. Galbraith, *The Affluent Society,* 1958, pp. 98-120.

25. Summer H. Slichter, James J. Healy, and E. Robert Livernash, *op. cit.,* p. 338, footnote 24. The validity of this position is questionable, however.

CHAPTER III

1. American Institute of Management, *The Corporate Director,* October, 1955, p. 1.

2. American Institute of Management, *Bulletin,* April, 1956, p. 1.

3. *Ibid.*

4. United States Industrial Commission, *Final Report,* Volume 19, 1902, p. 817.

5. United States Commissioner of Labor, *Eleventh Special Report: Regulation and Restriction of Output,* 1904, p. 122.

6. John Mitchell, *Organized Labor,* 1903, p. 255.

7. Max Weber, *Gesammelte Aufsatze zur Soziologie und Sozialpolitik,* 1924 (see Georges Friedmann, *Industrial Society,* 1955, p. 281). Weber, however, is mainly concerned with wage rate changes.

8. Charles S. Myers, *Mind and Work,* 1920, p. 116.

9. Stanley B. Mathewson, *Restriction of Output among Unorganized Workers,* 1931, pp. 11, 163.

10. International Labour Office, *Higher Productivity in Manufacturing Industries (Studies and Reports, New Series, No. 38),* 1954, p. 20.

11. John Martin, "Do Trade Unions Limit Output?" *Political Science Quarterly*, September, 1902, p. 371.

12. *Ibid.*, pp. 372-73; United States Industrial Commission, *Reports*, Volume 17, 1901, p. lx.

13. *Fortune*, May, 1955, p. 59.

14. New York State Joint Legislative Committee on Housing, *Final Report (Legislative Document No. 48)*, 1923, pp. 37-46.

15. Sumner H. Slichter, James J. Healy, and E. Robert Livernash, *The Impact of Collective Bargaining on Management*, 1960, p. 371.

16. John Mitchell, *op. cit.*, pp. 254, 255, 259.

17. Samuel Gompers, *Seventy Years of Life and Labor*, Volume 1, 1925, p. 47.

18. Samuel Gompers, "Who Limits Output?" *International Molders Journal*, November, 1919, p. 879.

19. *The Bridge Men's Magazine*, April, 1929, p. 228.

20. United Mine Workers of America, *Proceedings of the Constitutional Convention*, Volume 1, 1940, p. 287.

21. Bill Davidson, "Fear of Automation," *Look*, April 25, 1961, p. 76.

22. The figures used in this section have been taken from releases of the American Institute of Public Opinion. Generally they are reported by the press.

23. *The Iron Age*, March 28, 1946, p. 101.

24. *New York Herald Tribune*, April 20, 1962, p. 14:2.

25. 48 Stat. 204-05 (1933).

26. Sidney Lens, "Unions and Featherbedding," *The Commonweal*, September 30, 1960, pp. 7, 9.

27. *Time*, June 7, 1963, p. 96.

28. Alan Gladstone, "Redundancy and Dismissal in Europe— (II)," *International and Comparative Law Quarterly, Supplementary Publication No. 5*, 1962, p. 64.

29. *The Wall Street Journal*, August 18, 1959, p. 1:8; *Newsweek*, September 21, 1959, p. 102.

30. More detailed analysis of the breakdown of featherbedding costs in the railroad industry is found on pp. 82-83, 89.

31. Sumner H. Slichter, James J. Healy, and E. Robert Livernash, *op. cit.*, p. 333. Edward F. Denison estimates that the

elimination of all formal obstacles imposed by unions against use of the most efficient production practices would add a tenth of a percent to the rate of growth over a ten-year period or a twentieth of a percent over twenty years; see Edward F. Denison, *The Sources of Economic Growth in the United States,* 1962, pp. 195-96, 278.

32. F. H. Happold, "Redundancy, Industry and the Unions," *The Statist,* October 12, 1962, p. 105.

CHAPTER IV

1. Kent T. Healy, "The Problem—Rational and Effective Allocation of Resources," *The Annals of the American Academy of Political and Social Science,* January, 1963, p. 44.

2. Marvin L. Fair and Ernest W. Williams, Jr., *Economics of Transportation,* 1950, p. 618.

3. United States Eight-Hour Commission, *Report,* 1918.

4. Sumner H. Slichter, *Union Policies and Industrial Management,* 1941, p. 195.

5. United States Office of Defense Transportation, *Release ODT-57,* January 29, 1943.

6. United States Emergency Board No. 109, *Report to the President,* March 25, 1955, pp. 32, 35.

7. For a discussion of the impact of state full-crew laws on the employment of railroad operating workers, see pp. 175-80.

8. They were introduced in yard service in 1925.

9. The term "helper" was used in connection with work on electric locomotives and was carried over into diesel operations as "fireman (helper)."

10. United States Emergency Board, *Report to the President,* May 21, 1943 (To investigate . . . the proper manning on diesel . . . locomotives).

11. United States Emergency Board No. 68, *Report to the President,* April 11, 1949; United States Emergency Board No. 70, *Report to the President,* September 19, 1949.

12. Canada Royal Commission on Employment of Firemen on Diesel Locomotives in Freight and Yard Service on the Canadian Pacific Railway, *Report,* 1958. Several other relatively minor questions were also considered by the Commission.

13. *Ibid.,* p. 25.

14. Norman Coates, "Are Firemen Required on Diesel Locomotives?" *I L Research,* Spring, 1960, p. 14.

15. Morris A. Horowitz, "The Diesel Firemen Issue on the
Railroads," *Industrial and Labor Relations Review,* July, 1960,
p. 556.

16. *Railroad Passenger Train Deficit,* 306 ICC 480 (1959).

17. *The New York Times,* February 12, 1959, p. 16:1-2.

18. Morris A. Horowitz, *Manpower Utilization in the Railroad
Industry,* 1960, p. 55.

19. See United States Presidential Railroad Commission, *Re-
port,* 1962; four appendix volumes were issued: Volume 1—
Index-Digest to the Record of the Commission's Hearings;
Volume 2—*Pay Structure Study, Railroad Operating Employees;*
Volume 3—*Studies Relating to Railroad Operating Employees;*
Volume 4—*Studies Relating to Collective Bargaining Agreements
and Practices Outside the Railroad Industry.*

20. J. Handly Wright, "Featherbedding: Pitfall on the Path
of Progress," *The Commercial and Financial Chronicle,* August
13, 1959, p. 25.

21. George E. Leighty, "Railroad Propaganda Ignores the
Facts," *AFL-CIO American Federationist,* December, 1959, p. 6.

22. Gilbert Burck, "The Great Featherbed Fight," *Fortune,*
March, 1960, p. 202.

23. Alton F. Zimmerman, *Dissent to the Report of the Presidential Railroad Commission,* February 28, 1962, p. 15.

24. *Brotherhood of Locomotive Engineers* v. *Baltimore and
Ohio Railroad Company,* 310 F.2d 503, CA 7 (1962).

25. See 310 F.2d 513, CA 7 (1962).

26. 372 U.S. 284 (1963).

27. *Railroads* v. *Operating Brotherhoods,* 40 LA 609 (1963).

28. United States Special Subcommittee of the President's
Advisory Committee on Labor-Management Policy, *Report to
the President on the Railroad Rules Dispute,* July 19, 1963
(offset)

29. *The New York Times,* July 23, 1963, p. 12:2.

30. United States Senate, Committee on Labor and Public
Welfare, *Labor Dispute between Railroad Carriers and Four*

Operating Railroad Brotherhoods (Hearings), 82nd Congress, 1st Session, 1951, pp. 780-81.

31. 77 Stat. 132 (1963); see *The New York Times*, August 28, 1963, p. 23:1.

32. *Railroads* v. *Operating Brotherhoods*, 41 LA 673 (1963).

33. *The New York Times*, January 9, 1964, p. 63:1 and February 21, 1964, p. 16:8; see *Brotherhood of Locomotive Firemen and Enginemen* v. *Chicago, Burlington & Quincy Railroad Company*, 225 F.Supp. 11 (1964), affirmed 55 LRRM 2517, CA DC (1964).

34. United States Emergency Board No. 70, *Report to the President*, September 19, 1949.

35. *Brotherhood of Locomotive Firemen and Enginemen* v. *Southern Railway Company*, 217 F.Supp. 58 (1963); see also 212 F.Supp. 465 (1963).

36. *Labor*, April 13, 1963, pp. 1:4, 2:3.

37. *Ibid.*, May 11, 1963, p. 1:3-5. See also *United States* v. *Florida East Coast Railway Company*, 221 F.Supp. 325 (1963).

38. *Ibid.*, July 13, 1963, p. 4:3-4.

39. *Ibid.*, September 7, 1963, p. 4:2.

40. *The Wall Street Journal*, July 3, 1963, p. 6:3.

CHAPTER V

1. *Order of Railroad Telegraphers* v. *Chicago & North Western Railway Company*, 362 U.S. 330 (1960) reversing 264 F.2d 254 (1959).

2. *Business Week*, September 22, 1962, p. 95.

3. *Chicago & North Western Railway Company*, 39 LA 361 (1962).

4. *The New York Times* (Western Edition), March 25, 1963, pp. 1:8, 8:6-7.

5. *The Journal of Commerce*, March 6, 1961, p. 9:3.

6. National Academy of Sciences—National Research Council, Maritime Research Advisory Committee, *Proposed Program for Maritime Administration Research*, Volume 2, 1960, p. 244.

7. *Ibid.*, Volume 1, p. 39.

8. *The Economist*, December 15, 1962, p. 1132.

9. *The New York Times*, April 29, 1962, p. 88:2-4.

10. United States Emergency Board No. 133, *Report to the President*, December 10, 1960.

11. *The New York Times*, January 18, 1961, p. 24:7-8.

12. Bill Davidson, "Fear of Automation," *Look*, April 25, 1961, p. 70.

13. United States Railroad Marine Workers Commission, *Report*, June, 1962.

14. *The New York Times*, January 23, 1961, p. 15:5 and January 30, 1961, p. 1:4.

15. United States Emergency Board No. 134, *Report to the President*, March 6, 1961.

16. *The New York Times*, April 5, 1961, p. 74:2-3 and April 12, 1961, p. 81:6.

17. United States Railroad Lighter Captains Commission, *Report*, July, 1962.

18. Thomas Kennedy, *Automation Funds and Displaced Workers*, 1962, p. 75.

19. Max D. Kossoris, "Working Rules in West Coast Longshoring," *Monthly Labor Review*, January, 1961, pp. 1-10.

20. *The New York Times*, May 27, 1963, p. 15:2.

21. Lincoln Fairley, "The ILWU-PMA Mechanization and Modernization Agreement," *Labor Law Journal*, July, 1961, p. 669.

22. Lester Velie, "That Empty Chair by the Featherbed," *The Reader's Digest*, April, 1963, p. 100.

23. *The New York Times*, May 27, 1963, p. 15:3.

24. *Ibid.*, March 14, 1961, p. 69:4; *Business Week*, March 25, 1961, pp. 56, 58.

25. See Thomas Kennedy, *op. cit.*, pp. 102-11.

26. *The Brooklyn Longshoreman*, May-June, 1963, p. 2:1-2.

27. *Business Week*, September 15, 1962, p. 116.

28. James R. Macdonald, " 'Featherbed' Fears," *The Wall Street Journal*, October 3, 1962, p. 1:1.

29. *Ibid.*, p. 27:2.

30. Benjamin R. Miller, *Our Central States Labor Relations Experiment in Retrospect*, 1955, p. 10 (Special Report before the

Board of Governors of the Regular Common Carrier Conference of American Trucking Associations).

31. *Monthly Labor Review,* February, 1961, p. 187.

32. *Business Week,* April 21, 1962, p. 138; *The New York Times,* March 29, 1962, p. 52:5.

33. See Emerson P. Schmidt, *Industrial Relations in Urban Transportation,* 1937, pp. 244-47.

34. *City of Shreveport* v. *Shreveport Railways Company,* 38 F.2d 945, CA 5 (1930), cert. denied, 281 U.S. 763 (1930). The ordinance had been upheld, *Sullivan* v. *City of Shreveport,* 251 U.S. 169 (1919).

35. See *Fifth Avenue Coach Company,* 4 LA 548 (1946).

36. *The New York Times,* August 6, 1958, pp. 1:1, 50:2.

37. United States National Labor Board, *Decisions, Part II,* 1934, p. 21 (The Air Line Pilots' Wage Dispute, No. 83).

38. United States National Mediation Board, *Determination of Craft or Class,* Volume 3, 1961, p. 58.

39. United States President, *Report by the Commission . . . to Consider Differences . . . between . . . Air Carriers and . . . Their Employees,* 1961, p. 10.

40. A representation election held subsequently, which resulted in 1,682 votes for the ALPA and 58 for the FEIA, led to certification of the pilots' union. The flight engineers sought to challenge the determination of the NMB in the courts, but without success; see *UNA Chapter, FEIA* v. *National Mediation Board,* 294 F.2d 905, CA DC (1961).

41. United States Emergency Board No. 120, *Report to the President,* July 21, 1958, p. 52.

42. United States President, *op. cit.,* p. 20.

43. *The New York Times,* June 2, 1962, p. 46:6.

44. *Harper's Magazine,* November, 1962, p. 6.

45. United States Emergency Board No. 142, *Report to the President,* December 15, 1961; United States Emergency Board No. 143, *Report to the President,* December 10, 1961; United States Emergency Board No. 144, *Report to the President,* May 1, 1962; United States Emergency Board No. 146, *Report to the President,* May 1, 1962.

46. *Flight Engineers International Association, EAL Chapter* v. *Eastern Air Lines,* 208 F.Supp. 182 (1962) affirmed 307 F.2d 510, CA 2 (1962); see also 311 F.2d 745, CA 2 (1963).

47. *Pan American World Airways* v. *Flight Engineers International Association,* 306 F.2d 840, CA 2 (1962).

48. *The New York Times,* April 26, 1963, p. 70:1.

49. The ALPA contested the right of the National Mediation Board to conduct an election among pilots of American Airlines requested by the dissident group on April 24, 1963 for the purpose of determining the appropriate bargaining representative. See *Air Line Pilots Association* v. *National Mediation Board,* 220 F.Supp. 729 (1963), 220 F.Supp. 730 (1963), and 53 LRRM 2785 CA DC (1963).

50. *Ruby, Air Line Pilots Association* v. *American Airlines,* 54 LRRM 2020, 2042 (1963), affirmed 55 LRRM 2407, CA 2 (1964); part of the decision was affirmed at 323 F.2d 248, CA 2 (1963). The district court was concerned with the issues involving the relationships between the carrier and the two unions of pilots as well as those between the carrier and the FEIA.

CHAPTER VI

1. For specific examples given by Thornton, see above, p. 25.

2. William Haber, *Industrial Relations in the Building Industry,* 1930, pp. 197-237.

3. *Time,* February 17, 1958, p. 90.

4. Sumner H. Slichter, *Union Policies and Industrial Management,* 1941, p. 179.

5. United States Industrial Commission, *Report,* Volume 8, 1901, pp. xix-xx.

6. New York State Joint Legislative Committee on Housing, *Final Report (Legislative Document No. 48),* 1923, p. 19.

7. *Ibid.,* pp. 26, 30-31.

8. *Ibid.,* p. 37.

9. *The New York Times,* November 12, 1922, Section 10, p. 1:1.

10. "Digest of Material on Technological Changes, Productivity of Labor, and Labor Displacement," *Monthly Labor Review,* November, 1932, p. 1033; see also *Ibid.,* November, 1924, pp. 1-5.

11. United States Congress, Joint Committee on Housing, *Report of Hon. Joseph R. McCarthy, Vice Chairman,* 80th Con-

gress, 2nd Session, 1948, p. 9; see also United States Congress, *Housing America (House Document No. 629)*, 80th Congress, 2nd Session, 1948, pp. 38-44.

12. United States Congress, Joint Committee on Housing, *Cooperation by Labor in Solving the Housing Problem*, 1948, pp. 10-14.

13. See United States Congress, *Congressional Record*, Volume 93, Part 13, 80th Congress, 1st Session, 1947, pp. A4839-A4841.

14. *United States* v. *Glaziers' Local No. 27*, 35 CCH Labor Cases 97692 (1958).

15. *The New York Times*, February 8, 1958, p. 9:5-6.

16. United States Senate, *Report No. 1312*, 87th Congress, 2nd Session, 1962, p. 43.

17. *The Economist*, May 20, 1961, p. 783.

18. William Haber and Harold M. Levinson, *Labor Relations and Productivity in the Building Trades*, 1956, pp. 196-97, 250.

19. See Frank Chodorov, "Featherbedding: Robbery Made Legal," *Human Events*, April 1, 1959, Article Section, p. 1; James J. Butler, "Let's Eliminate Preposterous Featherbedding," *The Magazine of Wall Street*, June 6, 1959, p. 361; and Dickson Hartwell, "Low-Down on the Slowdown," *Collier's*, November 8, 1947, p. 20.

20. "Who's in the Featherbed?" *Fortune*, February, 1957, p. 206.

21. "Featherbedding: Fact and Fancy," *Engineering News-Record*, April 30, 1959, p. 82.

22. Royal E. Montgomery, *Industrial Relations in the Chicago Building Trades*, 1927, pp. 153-54.

23. Dickson Hartwell, *op. cit.*, p. 21.

24. See Walter Galenson, *The CIO Challenge to the AFL*, 1960, pp. 521-26.

25. *The New York Times*, February 8, 1954, p. 13:2; see also Hilton Gregory, "Labor Rules," *The Reader's Digest*, December, 1933, pp. 6-7.

26. Alfred Steinberg, "Can We Get Rid of Featherbedding?" *The Reader's Digest*, January, 1962, p. 143.

27. *The New York Times*, February 8, 1954, p. 13:6.

28. John R. Commons, *Labor and Administration*, 1913, p. 323.

29. *International Musician, Supplement*, June, 1911, p. 2.

30. Vern Countryman, "The Organized Musicians: I," *The University of Chicago Law Review*, Autumn, 1948, pp. 79-80.

31. *The New York Times*, February 9, 1954, p. 14:4.

32. Robert D. Leiter, *The Musicians and Petrillo*, 1953, p. 177. Problems of technological displacement among musicians are fully discussed in this study.

33. Joseph A. Padway, "The Musicians' Case," *American Federationist*, September, 1944, p. 12.

34. *Electrical Transcription Manufacturers*, 16 War Labor Reports 391 (1944).

35. *National Labor Relations Board* v. *E. C. Atkins & Company*, 331 U.S. 403 (1947).

36. United States House of Representatives, Special Subcommittee of the Committee on Education and Labor, *Musicians Performance Trust Funds (Hearings)*, 84th Congress, 2nd Session, 1956, p. 3; see also *Report*.

37. Thomas Kennedy, *Automation Funds and Displaced Workers*, 1962, pp. 61-62.

38. United States House of Representatives, *Report No. 1508*, 79th Congress, 2nd Session, 1946, p. 3.

39. *International Typographical Union*, 86 NLRB 959-60 (1949).

40. Woodruff Randolph, "Reproduction in the Printing and Publishing Industry," *Labor Law Journal*, May, 1953, pp. 307-08.

41. 86 NLRB 1026 (1949).

42. Woodruff Randolph, *op. cit.*, p. 310.

43. 86 NLRB 1027, footnote 79 (1949).

44. *The Typographical Journal*, July, 1961, Table 46, p. 53s.

45. It should be noted that in the larger metropolitan areas, work is departmentalized and bogus is set only by employees on the advertising side of the composing room. See 86 NLRB 1025, footnote 74 (1949).

46. Paul Jacobs, *Dead Horse and the Featherbird*, 1962, pp. 17-18.

47. *The Typographical Journal*, October, 1960, pp. 83c-94c and December, 1960, p. 232.

48. For example, in 1956 *The New York Times* sent full-sized facsimile editions of its paper from New York City to San Francisco by television microwave relay circuit.

49. *Encyclopaedia Britannica,* Volume 21, p. 912A.

50. *Collier's Encyclopedia,* Volume 17, p. 458.

51. Richard Severo, "Automation and the News Strike," *The Reporter,* March 14, 1963, p. 30.

52. *Ibid.,* p. 31.

53. Elizabeth F. Baker, *Displacement of Men by Machines,* 1933, pp. 130-61, 184.

54. *Editor & Publisher,* April 30, 1960, p. 42.

55. Jules Backman, "The Size of Crews," *Labor Law Journal,* September, 1961, p. 810.

56. *Bejae Printing Company,* 141 NLRB 1127 (1963).

57. *Philadelphia Inquirer,* 142 NLRB 36 (1963).

58. *The New York Times,* July 21, 1963, Section 4, p. 2:1.

59. Jules Backman, "Featherbedding Hurts You," *Nation's Business,* November, 1959, p. 40.

60. *Monthly Labor Review,* December, 1959, p. 1331.

61. *The New York Times,* June 21, 1963, pp. 1:8, 59:2-3. Since average seniority varies widely among the companies, relatively equal costs are imposed if the basis of extended vacations is half the employees rather than a specified number of years of service.

62. *The Wall Street Journal,* February 28, 1962, p. 1:1.

CHAPTER VII

1. *Hopkins* v. *Oxley Stave Company,* 83 Fed. 912, CA 8 (1897), affirming 72 Fed. 695 (1896).

2. Charles O. Gregory, *Labor and the Law,* 1961, p. 112.

3. *Ibid.,* p. 528.

4. *Duplex Printing Press Company* v. *Deering,* 254 U.S. 443 (1921); *Bedford Cut Stone Company* v. *Journeymen Stone Cutters' Association,* 274 U.S. 37 (1927).

5. Thurman W. Arnold, *The Bottlenecks of Business,* 1940, pp. 42, 206, 249-53.

6. Thurman Arnold, "Labor against Itself," *Cosmopolitan*, November, 1943, p. 122.

7. *United States* v. *Hutcheson*, 312 U.S. 219 (1941).

8. *United States* v. *United Brotherhood of Carpenters and Joiners*, 313 U.S. 539 (1941); *United States* v. *Building and Construction Trades Council*, 313 U.S. 539 (1941).

9. *United States* v. *International Hod Carriers and Common Laborers*, 313 U.S. 539 (1941), affirming 37 F.Supp. 191 (1941).

10. *United States* v. *American Federation of Musicians*, 318 U.S. 741 (1943), affirming 47 F.Supp. 304 (1942).

11. *Allen Bradley Company* v. *Local 3, I.B.E.W.*, 325 U.S. 797 (1945).

12. Sumner H. Slichter, *The Challenge of Industrial Relations*, 1947, p. 68.

13. *United States* v. *Compagna*, 146 F.2d 524, CA 2 (1944), cert. denied 324 U.S. 867 (1945); *Nick* v. *United States*, 122 F.2d 660, CA 8 (1941), cert. denied 314 U.S. 687 (1941).

14. *United States* v. *Local 807, Teamsters*, 315 U.S. 521 (1942).

15. *United States* v. *Green*, 350 U.S. 415 (1956) and 355 U.S. 871 (1957).

16. *United States* v. *Postma*, 242 F.2d 488, CA 2 (1957), cert. denied 354 U.S. 922 (1957).

17. *United States* v. *American Federation of Musicians*, 47 F.Supp. 304 (1942), affirmed 318 U.S. 741 (1943).

18. *United States* v. *Petrillo*, 332 U.S. 1 (1947), reversing 68 F.Supp. 845 (1946).

19. *United States* v. *Petrillo*, 75 F.Supp. 176 (1948).

20. *General Teleradio, Inc.* v. *Manuti*, 133 N.Y.S.2d 362 (N.Y. Sup. Ct.), 1954.

21. *Opera on Tour, Inc.* v. *Weber*, 285 N.Y. 348, 357 (1941).

22. *Lafayette Dramatic Productions, Inc.* v. *Ferentz*, 305 Mich. 193 (Mich. Sup. Ct.), 1943.

23. United States Congress, *Congressional Record*, Volume 93, Part 5, 80th Congress, 1st Session, 1947, p. 6441.

24. *American Newspaper Publishers Association* v. *N.L.R.B.*, 345 U.S. 100 (1953), affirming 193 F.2d 782, CA 7 (1951).

25. *N.L.R.B.* v. *Gamble Enterprises, Inc.*, 345 U.S. 117 (1953), reversing 196 F.2d 61, CA 6 (1952).

26. This decision was not published (case 19 CB 292, August 23, 1954).

27. *National Labor Relations Board* v. *Radio and Television Broadcast Engineers Union,* 364 U.S. 573 (1961).

28. *J. A. Jones Construction Company,* 135 NLRB 1402 (1962).

29. *P. Lorillard Company, Inc.,* 135 NLRB 1382 (1962).

30. *Frank P. Badolato and Son,* 135 NLRB 1392 (1962).

31. *American Radiator and Standard Sanitary Corporation,* 137 NLRB 1524 (1962).

32. *Joliet Contractors Assn.* v. *N.L.R.B.,* 202 F.2d 606, CA 7 (1953).

33. Printz Leather Company, 94 NLRB 1312 (1951).

34. *N.L.R.B.* v. *Cantrall,* 201 F.2d 853, CA 9 (1953), cert. denied 345 U.S. 996 (1953).

35. *Chicago, Rock Island, and Pacific Railway Company* v. *State of Arkansas,* 219 U.S. 453 (1911); *St. Louis, Iron Mountain, and Southern Railway Company* v. *State of Arkansas,* 240 U.S. 518 (1916); *Missouri Pacific Railroad Company* v. *Norwood,* 283 U.S. 249 (1931).

36. *Pennsylvania Railroad* v. *Driscoll,* 9 Atl.2d 621 (1939).

37. See Sumner H. Slichter, James J. Healy, and E. Robert Livernash, *The Impact of Collective Bargaining on Management,* 1960, pp. 322-29; see also "Railroad Legislation on Full Crew, Personnel, and Train Lengths," *Monthly Labor Review,* June, 1940, pp. 1429-33.

38. *Southern Pacific Company* v. *Arizona,* 325 U.S. 761 (1945).

39. The National City Bank of New York, *Monthly Letter on Economic Conditions,* February, 1949, p. 21.

40. Robert W. Purcell, *Special Report to the Governor on Problems of the Railroad and Bus Lines in New York State,* March 12, 1959, pp. 18-20.

41. New York State Legislative Document (1960), *Report of Investigation by the Public Service Commission of the Full Crew Laws Constituting Sections 54-a, 54-b, and 54-c of the Railroad Law,* January 26, 1960.

42. New York State Temporary State Commission on Economic Expansion, *Report: Steps Toward Economic Expansion in New York State,* 1960, pp. 14, 120-21.

43. *The Wall Street Journal,* March 28, 1963, p. 16:4.

44. *Railroad Passenger Train Deficit,* 306 ICC 454 (1959).

45. See John R. Van de Water, "Industrial Productivity and the Law: A Study of Work Restrictions," *Virginia Law Review,* February, 1957, pp. 166-69.

46. John V. Schappi, "Labor Law: Federal Regulation: Featherbedding," *Cornell Law Quarterly,* Fall, 1953, pp. 132-33.

CHAPTER VIII

1. Charles O. Gregory, *Labor and the Law,* 1961, p. 530.

2. Jean B. Say, *A Treatise on Political Economy,* Volume 1, 1814, p. 55, footnote (French edition). Later editions, however, suggested that prerogatives of inventors are invaded by governmental restrictions on use.

3. American Federation of Labor, *Report of Proceedings,* 1907, p. 286.

4. The American Assembly, Columbia University, *Automation and Technological Change,* 1962, pp. 125, 127.

5. United States National Resources Committee, *Technological Trends and National Policy,* 1937, p. vii.

6. Alton F. Zimmerman, *Dissent to the Report of the Presidential Railroad Commission,* February 28, 1962, p. 62.

7. See Arnold R. Weber, "The Interplant Transfer of Displaced Employees," in Gerald G. Somers, Edward L. Cushman, and Nat Weinberg, eds., *Adjusting to Technological Change,* 1963, pp. 95-143.

8. See Morse A. Cartwright, ed., *Unemployment and Adult Education,* 1931.

9. Harry Ober, *Trade-Union Policy and Technological Change* (United States Work Projects Administration, National Research Project, Report No. L-8), 1940, pp. 25-26.

10. William G. Caples, "Automation in Theory and Practice," *Business Topics,* Autumn, 1960, p. 16.

11. United States Department of Labor, Bureau of Labor Statistics, *Bulletin No. 1368 (Industrial Retraining Programs for Technological Change),* 1963, p. 6.

12. United States Coal Commission, *Report, Part 3*, 1925, pp. 1321-22.

13. *Ibid., Part 1*, 1925, p. 111.

14. See *Business Week*, March 31, 1962, pp. 50-52.

15. *Monthly Labor Review*, October, 1959, pp. 1109-10.

16. *The New York Times*, June 19, 1961, p. 18:5.

17. Thomas Kennedy, *Automation Funds and Displaced Workers*, 1962, pp. 158-59.

18. *The Wall Street Journal*, August 26, 1963, p. 5:5.

19. *The New York Times*, May 30, 1963, p. 22:1.

20. Charles O. Gregory, *op. cit.*, pp. 112-13.

21. The report was submitted to the President on January 11, 1962; see *Monthly Labor Review*, February, 1962, pp. 139-42 and *Business Week*, May 6, 1961, p. 28.

22. Phyllis Groom, "Retraining the Unemployed," *Monthly Labor Review*, September, 1961, p. 940.

23. 75 Stat. 47 (1961).

24. 76 Stat. 23 (1962).

25. 76 Stat. 872, 892-896 (1962).

26. See *Monthly Labor Review*, March, 1963, p. 244.

27. United States House of Representatives, Subcommittee on Unemployment and the Impact of Automation of the Committee on Education and Labor, *Report: Impact of Automation on Employment*, 87th Congress, 1st Session, 1961, pp. 20-21.

28. Bertil Olsson, "Policy Implications of Technological Change in Western Europe," in Gerald G. Somers, Edward L. Cushman, and Nat Weinberg, eds., *op. cit.*, p. 193.

BIBLIOGRAPHY

I. GENERAL SOURCES

The New York Times
The New York Times Index
Railway Age Weekly

II. BOOKS

The American Assembly, Columbia University, *Automation and Technological Change*, 1962

Baker, Elizabeth F., *Displacement of Men by Machines*, 1933

Barnett, George E., *Chapters on Machinery and Labor*, 1926

Cartwright, Morse A., ed., *Unemployment and Adult Education*, 1931

Federated American Engineering Societies, Committee on Elimination of Waste in Industry, *Waste in Industry*, 1921, pp. 18-20, 296-298

Haber, William, *Industrial Relations in the Building Industry*, 1930, pp. 197-237

Haber, William and Harold M. Levinson, *Labor Relations and Productivity in the Building Trades*, 1956, pp. 103-203, 242-251

Horowitz, Morris A., *Manpower Utilization in the Railroad Industry*, 1960

Industrial Relations Research Association, *Proceedings of the Fourteenth Annual Meeting*, 1961, pp. 377-423 (Part X: The Evolution of Work Rules and Their Effects on Employment—Jacob J. Kaufman, "Logic and Meaning of Work Rules on the Railroads," pp. 378-388; E. Robert Livernash, "The General Problem of Work Rules," pp. 389-398; Jack Stieber, "Work Rules and Practices in Mass Production Industries," pp. 399-412; Discussion—William Gomberg, David Kaplan, and Garth L. Mangum, pp. 413-423)

International Labour Office, *Higher Productivity in Manufacturing Industries (Studies and Reports, New Series, No. 38)*, 1954, pp. 15-42

226

Jacobs, Paul, *Dead Horse and the Featherbird,* 1962
Kennedy, Thomas, *Automation Funds and Displaced Workers,* 1962
Leiter, Robert D., *The Musicians and Petrillo,* 1953
Mathewson, Stanley B., *Restriction of Output Among Unorganized Workers,* 1931
Slichter, Sumner H., *Union Policies and Industrial Management,* 1941, pp. 164-281
Slichter, Sumner H., James J. Healy, and E. Robert Livernash, *The Impact of Collective Bargaining on Management,* 1960, pp. 317-371
Somers, Gerald G., Edward L. Cushman, and Nat Weinberg, eds., *Adjusting to Technological Change,* 1963
Zimmerman, Alton F., *Dissent to Report of the Presidential Railroad Commission,* February 28, 1962

III. MAGAZINE ARTICLES

Aaron, Benjamin, "Governmental Restraints on Featherbedding," *Stanford Law Review,* July, 1953, pp. 680-721
Ardzrooni, Leon, "The Philosophy of the Restriction of Output," *The Annals of the American Academy of Political and Social Science,* September, 1920, pp. 70-75
Arnold, Thurman W., "Labor's Hidden Holdup Men," *The Reader's Digest,* June, 1941, pp. 136-140
Backman, Jules, "Cushioning the Impact of Technological Change," *Labor Law Journal,* September, 1962, pp. 731-746
Backman, Jules, "Featherbedding Hurts You," *Nation's Business,* November, 1959, pp. 40-41, 79-81
Backman, Jules, "The Size of Crews," *Labor Law Journal,* September, 1961, pp. 805-815
Barden, John, "Railroad Labor Crisis," *The Nation,* September 12, 1959, pp. 128-133
Berg, Ivar and James Kuhn, "The Assumptions of Featherbedding," *Labor Law Journal,* April, 1962, pp. 277-283
Blum, Albert A., "Fourth Man Out—Background of the Flight Engineer—Airline Pilot Conflict," *Labor Law Journal,* August, 1962, pp. 649-657
Brach, William L., "Legislative Shackles on Featherbedding Practices," *Cornell Law Quarterly,* Winter, 1948, pp. 255-263
Brogan, Colm, "British Make-Work Takes a Blow," *National Review,* March 28, 1959, pp. 615-616

Brozen, Yale, "The Economics of Automation," *American Economic Review*, May, 1957, pp. 339-350

Burck, Gilbert, "The Great Featherbed Fight," *Fortune*, March, 1960, pp. 151-153, 198-202

Butler, James J., "Let's Eliminate Preposterous Featherbedding," *The Magazine of Wall Street*, June 6, 1959, pp. 329-331, 361-362

Coates, Norman, "Are Firemen Required on Diesel Locomotives?" *I L Research*, Spring, 1960, pp. 8-14

Cottrell, William F., "Death by Dieselization: A Case Study in the Reaction to Technological Change," *American Sociological Review*, June, 1951, pp. 358-365

Davidson, Bill, "Fear of Automation," *Look*, April 25, 1961, pp. 69-76

Daykin, Walter L., "Featherbedding," *Labor Law Journal*, November, 1956, pp. 699-710

Dickinson, William B., Jr., "Retraining for New Jobs," *Editorial Research Reports*, October 31, 1962, pp. 773-792

Doherty, Robert E., "Waste Not, Profit Not," *The Commonweal*, December 1, 1961, pp. 250-252

Edelman, Milton and Irving Kovarsky, "Featherbedding: Law and Arbitration," *Labor Law Journal*, April, 1959, pp. 233-246

Fairley, Lincoln, "The ILWU-PMA Mechanization and Modernization Agreement," *Labor Law Journal*, July, 1961, pp. 664-680

"Featherbedding and Taft-Hartley," *Columbia Law Review*, December, 1952, pp. 1020-1033

"Featherbedding and the Federal Anti-Racketeering Act," *The University of Chicago Law Review*, Autumn, 1958, pp. 150-164

Gladstone, Alan, "Redundancy and Dismissal in Europe—(II)," *International and Comparative Law Quarterly, Supplementary Publication No. 5*, 1962, pp. 58-69

Glazier, William, "Featherbedding vs. Automation," *The Nation*, September 10, 1960, pp. 131-133

Gomberg, William, "Featherbedding: An Assertion of Property Rights," *The Annals of the American Academy of Political and Social Science*, January, 1961, pp. 119-129

Gregory, Hilton, "Labor Rules," *The Reader's Digest*, December, 1933, pp. 5-10

Hartwell, Dickson, "Low-Down on the Slowdown," *Collier's*, November 8, 1947, pp. 20-21, 70-71

Henzey, William V., "Labor Problems in the Airline Industry," *Law and Contemporary Problems*, Winter, 1960, pp. 43-56

Hobsbawm, Eric J., "The Machine Breakers," *Past & Present,* February, 1952, pp. 57-70

Horowitz, Morris A., "The Diesel Firemen Issue on the Railroads," *Industrial and Labor Relations Review,* July, 1960, pp. 550-558

Horowitz, Morris A., "Featherbedding: The Specter in Future Collective Bargaining?" *Labor Law Journal,* January, 1960, pp. 19-22, 58

Horowitz, Morris A., "The Railroads' Dual System of Payment: A Make-Work Rule?" *Industrial and Labor Relations Review,* January, 1955, pp. 177-194

Kaiser, Henry, "The Folklore of Featherbedding," *De Paul Law Review,* Spring-Summer, 1954, pp. 169-183

Kaufman, Jacob J., "Working Rules in the Railroad Industry," *Labor Law Journal,* December, 1954, pp. 819-827

Killingsworth, Charles C., "The Modernization of West Coast Longshore Work Rules," *Industrial and Labor Relations Review,* April, 1962, pp. 295-306; "West Coast Longshore Work Rules," *Industrial and Labor Relations Review,* October, 1962, pp. 134-136 (Communication by Lincoln Fairley; Reply by Charles C. Killingsworth)

Kuehnl, Neil R., "How the Goof-Off Gulps Your Building Dollars," *Better Homes and Gardens,* April, 1959, pp. 64-65, 121-122

Kuhn, James and Ivar Berg, "The Trouble with Labor is 'Featherbedding,'" *Columbia University Forum,* Spring, 1960, pp. 22-26

Leighty, George E., "Railroad Propaganda Ignores the Facts," *AFL-CIO American Federationist,* December, 1959, pp. 4-6, 28-30

Lens, Sidney, "Unions and Featherbedding," *The Commonweal,* September 30, 1960, pp. 7-10

Lunde, Anders S., "The American Federation of Musicians and the Recording Ban," *The Public Opinion Quarterly,* Spring, 1948, pp. 45-56

Macdonald, James R., "'Featherbed' Fears," *The Wall Street Journal,* October 3, 1962, pp. 1:1, 27:2-3

Manuel, Frank E., "The Luddite Movement in France," *The Journal of Modern History,* June, 1938, pp. 180-211

Marshall, Joseph R., "Featherbedding Pads the Bill," *Dun's Review and Modern Industry,* June, 1960, pp. 111-125

Martin, John, "Do Trade Unions Limit Output?" *Political Science Quarterly,* September, 1902, pp. 369-380

Masse, Benjamin L., "Featherbedding on the Railroads?" *America,* January 2, 1960, pp. 392-394

McIntyre, William R., "Featherbedding and Union Work Rules," *Editorial Research Reports,* November 4, 1959, pp. 813-832

Morris, Joe A., "What Is Railroad 'Featherbedding'?" *The Saturday Evening Post,* February 27, 1960, pp. 32-33, 69-74

Northrup, Herbert R., "Plain Facts about Featherbedding," *Personnel,* July-August, 1958, pp. 54-60

Oram, James W., Philip H. Scheiding, and E. Robert Livernash, "The 'Work Practices' Issue—A Current Labor Problem," *Management Record,* May, 1960, pp. 18-27

Patric, John and Frank J. Taylor, "'Featherbedding' Hampers The War Effort," *The Reader's Digest,* March, 1943, pp. 25-29

Pitzele, Merlyn S., "Labor's Featherbeds—What They Cost You," *American Magazine,* March, 1946, pp. 48-49, 149-151

"Pressure Mounts against Featherbedding," *Nation's Business,* June, 1959, pp. 96-102

Randle, C. Wilson, "Restrictive Practices of Unionism," *The Southern Economic Journal,* October, 1948, pp. 171-183

Randolph, Woodruff, "Reproduction in the Printing and Publishing Industry," *Labor Law Journal,* May, 1953, pp. 307-310, 378-383

Severo, Richard, "Automation and the News Strike," *The Reporter,* March 14, 1963, pp. 29-32

Shelton, Willard, "Featherbedding," *New Republic,* July 28, 1947, pp. 30-31

Simler, Norman J., "The Economics of Featherbedding," *Industrial and Labor Relations Review,* October, 1962, pp. 111-121

Steinberg, Alfred, "Can We Get Rid Of Featherbedding?" *The Reader's Digest,* January, 1962, pp. 141-145

Thornbury, Kenneth F., "The Crisis on Job Control: A Union View," *Western Business Review,* February, 1960, pp. 31-39

"Three Men on an Iron Horse," *Fortune,* May, 1949, pp. 191-192

Tobin, Richard L., "Lets Get Rid of 'Bogus'—Now!" *Saturday Review,* February 11, 1961, pp. 79-80

Van de Water, John R., "A Fresh Look at Featherbedding," *Baylor Law Review,* Spring, 1955, pp. 138-160

Van de Water, John R., "The Broader Effects of the Taft-Hartley Act on Make-Work Practices in Industry," *U.C.L.A. Law Review,* December, 1955, pp. 27-54

Van de Water, John R., "Control of Featherbedding by the Secondary Boycott Ban," *Labor Law Journal*, September, 1955, pp. 633-653, 665

Van de Water, John R., "Industrial Productivity and the Law: A Study of Work Restrictions," *Virginia Law Review*, February, 1957, pp. 155-196

Van de Water, John R., "Influences of the Common Law on Make-Work Practices in Industry," *Labor Law Journal*, February, 1955, pp. 87-102, 126

Velie, Lester, "That Empty Chair By The Featherbed," *The Reader's Digest*, April, 1963, pp. 97-102

Walker, Jerome H., " 'Bogus' Has a Long History and ITU Seeks to Extend It," *Editor & Publisher*, April 23, 1960, pp. 24, 82-86, 92-94

Waterhouse, Warren C., "Featherbedding," *Western Business Review*, February, 1960, pp. 23-30

Weinstein, Paul A., "Featherbedding: A Theoretical Analysis," *The Journal of Political Economy*, August, 1960, pp. 379-387; Norman J. Simler, "Weinstein on Featherbedding: A Comment," *The Journal of Political Economy*, June, 1962, pp. 299-301

Wess, Harold B., "Can We Solve Our Economy's Most Dangerous Problem?" *The Reader's Digest*, October, 1957, pp. 54-56

"Who's in the Featherbed?" *Fortune*, February, 1957, p. 206

Wood, Norman J., "The Wisdom of Outlawing Featherbedding," *Labor Law Journal*, December, 1955, pp. 821-824

Wright, J. Handly, "Featherbedding: Pitfall on the Path of Progress," *The Commercial and Financial Chronicle*, August 13, 1959, pp. 15, 24-25

IV.   GOVERNMENT DOCUMENTS

Backman, Jules, *The Economics of Railroad Make-Work Rules and Featherbedding*, 1961 (United States Presidential Railroad Commission, Carriers Exhibit No. 10)

Canada Royal Commission on Employment of Firemen on Diesel Locomotives in Freight and Yard Service on the Canadian Pacific Railway, *Report*, 1958

"Digest of Material on Technological Changes, Productivity of Labor, and Labor Displacement," *Monthly Labor Review*, November, 1932, pp. 1031-1057

Fairley, Lincoln, "Problems of the West Coast Longshore Mechanization Agreement," *Monthly Labor Review*, June, 1961, pp. 597-600

Gomberg, William, "The Work Rule Problem and Property Rights in the Job," *Monthly Labor Review*, June, 1961, pp. 595-596

Gourvitch, Alexander, *Survey of Economic Theory on Technological Change and Employment* (United States Work Projects Administration, National Research Project, Report No. G-6), 1940

Groom, Phyllis, "Retraining the Unemployed," *Monthly Labor Review*, September, 1961, pp. 939-943 (II—Federal and State Legislation on Retraining)

Kossoris, Max D., "Working Rules in West Coast Longshoring," *Monthly Labor Review*, January, 1961, pp. 1-10

New York State Legislative Document (1960), *Report of Investigation by the Public Service Commission of the Full Crew Laws Constituting Sections 54-a, 54-b, and 54-c of the Railroad Law*, January 26, 1960

Ober, Harry, *Trade-Union Policy and Technological Change* (United States Work Projects Administration, National Research Project, Report No. L-8), 1940

"Railroad Legislation on Full Crew, Personnel, and Train Lengths," *Monthly Labor Review*, June, 1940, pp. 1429-1434

Stern, Bernhard J., "Resistances to the Adoption of Technological Innovations," United States National Resources Committee, *Technological Trends and National Policy*, 1937, pp. 39-66

United States Commission on Industrial Relations, *Final Report and Testimony*, Volume 1, 1916 (United States Senate Document No. 415, 64th Congress, 1st Session), pp. 127-143, 238-240

United States Commissioner of Labor, *Eleventh Special Report: Regulation and Restriction of Output*, 1904 (United States House of Representatives Document No. 734, 58th Congress, 2nd Session)

United States Commissioner of Labor, *Thirteenth Annual Report (Hand and Machine Labor)*, Volume 1, 1899

United States House of Representatives, Committee on Education and Labor, *Restrictive Union Practices of the American Federation of Musicians (Hearings)*, 80th Congress, 2nd Session, 1948

United States House of Representatives, Special Subcommittee of the Committee on Education and Labor, *Musicians Performance Trust Funds (Hearings)*, 84th Congress, 2nd Session, 1956

United States House of Representatives, Special Subcommittee of the Committee on Education and Labor, *Musicians Performance Trust Funds: Report*, 84th Congress, 2nd Session, 1956

United States House of Representatives, Subcommittee of the Committee on Labor, *Investigation of Unemployment Caused by Labor-Saving Devices in Industry (Hearings)*, 74th Congress, 2nd Session, 1936

United States Industrial Commission, *Reports*, Volume 17, 1901, pp. lviii-lxii (Labor Organizations, Labor Disputes, and Arbitration)

United States President, *Report by the Commission Established by Executive Order 10921 Dated February 21, 1961, as Amended to Consider Differences that Have Arisen between Certain Air Carriers and Certain of Their Employees*, May 24, 1961; *Supplemental Report*, October 17, 1961

United States Presidential Railroad Commission, *Report*, 1962; four appendix volumes were issued: Volume 1—*Index-Digest to the Record of the Commission's Hearings;* Volume 2—*Pay Structure Study, Railroad Operating Employees;* Volume 3—*Studies Relating to Railroad Operating Employees;* Volume 4—*Studies Relating to Collective Bargaining Agreements and Practices Outside the Railroad Industry*

United States Railroad Lighter Captains Commission, *Report*, July, 1962

United States Railroad Marine Workers Commission, *Report*, June, 1962

United States Special Subcommittee of the President's Advisory Committee on Labor-Management Policy, *Report to the President on the Railroad Rules Dispute*, July 19, 1963 (offset); see 53 LRRM 39-43 (appendices not included)

INDEX